*To Carol*
*Best wishes*
*Anthony Bill*

"I can recommend Congressional Chronicles *as an entertaining collection of lively, amusing and informative anecdotes about people and events in the history of Congress.*

"I am impressed with the amount of research that went into compiling these stories, particularly its use of previously unpublished oral histories from the Library of Congress and National Archives. Other vignettes are drawn from diaries, memoirs and newspaper accounts. They are factually based and are often as insightful as they are humorous.

"The volume presents the human side of the legislative branch, in a manner that should prove appealing to any visitor to Washington who is curious about what happens behind the city's marble facades."

Donald A. Ritchie, Ph.D.
Associate Historian
U.S. Senate Historical Office, Washington, D.C.

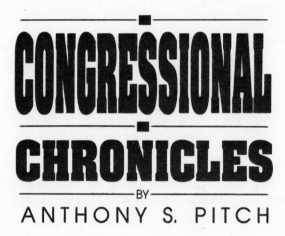

# CONGRESSIONAL CHRONICLES

BY

## ANTHONY S. PITCH

Mino Publications, Inc.
Potomac, MD

Published by

Mino Publications, Inc.
9009 Paddock Lane
Potomac, MD. 20854


Acknowledgment for permission to reprint from previously published
material and from unpublished documents is found on page 191.



Library of Congress Catalog Card No. 90-91538

ISBN 0-931719-07-0

Printed in the United States of America

*To all past, present and future members of Congress*
*May they long continue to entertain and amuse*

————⧠————

# CONTENTS

# ACKNOWLEDGMENTS

————□————

Unqualified appreciation goes first and foremost to my wife, Marion, and to my son and daughter, Michael and Nomi for their patience and understanding during the research and writing.

Gregory C. Harness, Head Reference Librarian at the U.S. Senate Library, where most of this research was done, provided invaluable assistance with unfailing grace and good humor, even though burdened with hectic daily schedules. The extraordinary special consideration extended to me was of such a nature that it quickened the investigative process beyond measure.

Dr. Donald A. Ritchie, Associate Historian, U.S. Senate Historical Office, was extremely generous in sharing some of his encylcopedic knowledge of Congress. I am particularly indebted to him for reading through the completed manuscript. Any errors that may have slipped through are mine, for which I take full responsibility.

Three dedicated professionals in the Office of the U.S. Senate Curator assisted with a warmth and friendliness which will long be remembered, particularly during research of the unpublished papers of Isaac Bassett, a Senate employee from 1831 until 1895. My deep gratitude to Scott M. Strong, Museum Specialist, who also guided me around the floor of the Senate chamber; John B. Odell, Registrarial Assistant; and Diane K. Skvarla, Associate Curator.

My thanks to Dr. Bruce A. Ragsdale, Associate Historian in the Office of the Historian, U.S. House of Representatives, who was always available for information and verification of minutiae.

Special thanks are due to a number of people for their expeditious permission to use rewritten passages from numerous unpublished oral histories listed under Bibliography on pages 198-199. My gratitude to former congressman Jed Johnson, Jr., Executive Director, U.S. Association of Former Members of Congress; Noraleen Young, Reference Librarian, Manuscript Section, Indiana Division, Indiana State Library; and Reid S. Derr, Interim Director, Mississippi Oral History Program, University of Southern Mississippi.

A number of officials were most helpful in locating books, documents, microfilm reels and illustrations at the Library of Congress Manuscript, Microform, Prints and Photographs Divisions, and Photoduplication Service; the Martin Luther King, Jr. Library in Washington, D.C.; the Public Library in Rockville, MD.; and the New York Public Library Prints Division.

Karen Portik fulfilled all expectations for a multiplicity of page designs, supplemented by her lively sketches and caricatures. She also designed the arresting front and back covers.

-- *Anthony S. Pitch*

# HUMOR & WIT

---□---

*I never lack material for my humor column when Congress is in session.*

*--Will Rogers*

The family doctor should never have worn new shoes to Washington, D.C. In the office of former patient Rep. Phillip Landrum (D-Ga.), he objected to Medicare legislation. Landrum tried to explain its merits but the doctor wouldn't budge. At that moment Landrum noticed that the physician's new shoes were too tight and killing him. Mischievously, Landrum invited him to lunch at a faraway restaurant and deliberately set a fast clip to make the doctor hop and sweat. Years later, with most of the physicians back in Landrum's fold, the doctor who had hotfooted it to lunch invited Landrum to be his house guest. "I ain't coming over there because you might give me some sort of pill and I might not wake up," Landrum joked.

---□---

*They tell a story on Capitol Hill about the days when New Jersey politicians were tightly controlled by machine bosses. It was common for New Jersey congressmen to telephone back home for voting instructions. One day, during a key vote, a frustrated New Jersey congressman slammed down the phone. "What's the matter?" a colleague enquired. "Those stupid people up there in Jersey City!" fumed the legislator from New Jersey. "If they can't make up their minds I'm going to vote my conscience!"*

Tests made on living congressmen in 1933 showed that senators have heavier brains than representatives. A researcher found the average brain weight of 17 members of the House to be 50 ounces while 18 senators were each burdened with carrying a heavier load of 52 ounces of gray matter. Dr. Arthur MacDonald told the American Association for the Advancement of Science that he found out the brain weight by measuring the length, height and width of legislators' craniums. It was too much for one puzzled senator. "A little while ago, doctor, you were measuring criminals," he said. "Now you are measuring senators. What's the idea?" The answer? Physical characteristics pointed to future diseases and by taking preventive measures, congressmen might live a lot longer.

---

**S**en. Robert Hayne of South Carolina once turned on Daniel Webster and charged him with sleeping through two of his speeches. "Yes," Webster shot back, "I did sleep during the gentleman's speech, and I slept well. I also slept equally well on the speech to which I am now replying."

*Henrik Shipstead was something of an enigma to the political fraternity during the roaring twenties and a decade beyond. Neither a Republican nor a Democrat, Shipstead won three terms to the U.S. Senate on the Farmer-Labor ticket. How come the Minnesotan dentist remained so popular when he took lone wolf stands on so many issues? Politicos joked that when Shipstead prayed he always began: "Lord, this is Shipstead speaking."*

Practical joker Sen. Richard Coke filched several pages of a prepared speech just before an unsuspecting Sen. James George got up to deliver it. When George (D-Miss.) got to the missing pages he came to an awkward halt. Frantically, he turned over one page after the other in search of the continuation. Senators in the know had a good chuckle before Coke (D-Tex.) put George out of his misery by handing back the missing part.

*Visiting King George VI tried to be informal when he hosted a summer garden party at the British embassy in Washington in 1939. When South Carolina's senior Senator Ellison Smith was introduced, the shy monarch asked, "Cotton Ed Smith?" Cotton Ed, who got his nickname by running on a plank to protect cotton farmers, responded more down-to-earth than expected by slapping the incredulous king on the back. Then the South Carolinian greeted the Queen with his own version of southern charm - "Howdy, Majesty."*

*Perhaps the quickest wit ever to sit in the House of Representatives was William Jenner (R-Ind.) He excelled during a dreary speech by Rep. Glen Taylor (D-Idaho), who got a little bit more maudlin than usual. "When I was a little boy my father was an itinerant Baptist preacher," said Taylor. "He baptized 15,000 people in the great West. Why, he baptized me five times." At that, Jenner piped up, "Son-of-a-gun's waterlogged!"*

One of the highlights of J. Allen Frear's political career was the visit he made to his in-laws small town in Hartford, Wisconsin, shortly after his marriage to his wife, Esther. Frear, who represented Delaware in the Senate from 1949 to 1961, was a Democrat. Esther's family, like almost everyone in Hartford, was Republican to the hilt. At the party hosted by Frear's in-laws, everyone suddenly went silent. Frear was asked to stand in the middle of the room. "Now, friends," said Frear's father-in-law, "I want you to see and know what a Democrat is. You probably have never seen one before, but here is one!"

*Hardly a day passed without Allen Ellender exercising in the Senate gym. One day the Louisiana Democrat was drying himself after a workout and a swim when the bells rang for a vote. Reflexively, Ellender ran out, momentarily forgetting he was wrapped only in a towel. Fortunately for him a gym attendant stopped him as he made for the elevator.*

A distinguished senator and his wife gate-crashed a diplomatic dinner party by driving up to the wrong embassy. It happened in the mid 20th century to Sen. Ralph Flanders (R-Vt.). Invited to dine at the French embassy, Flanders and his wife mistakenly pulled up in front of the Portuguese mission and joined other dinner guests. The first hint that all was not right came when they were shown the seating plan and failed to find their names. Though they could not spot their host, the French ambassador, they were led off to join other guests on the terrace. Curiously, no-one spoke French. Beginning to feel slightly ill at ease, Flanders and his wife were saved by Gallic intuition. The French telephoned their Portugese neighbors asking if anyone had spotted their missing guests.

Three VIPs waited outside the Capitol to receive Ronald Reagan for his first inauguration as president. The newly elected Senate sergeant-at-arms, Howard Liebengood, turned anxiously to the majority leader, Sen. Howard Baker. "How do you greet these people?" asked Liebengood. "Watch Nordy, he knows," said Baker. Nordy Hoffman, the retiring sergeant-at-arms was a 6 ft. 3 in., 300 lb. former tackle and guard on Knute Rockne's winning 1929 and 1930 Notre Dame football team. When the president-elect's limousine pulled up a Secret Service agent opened the door and Reagan stepped out. Hoffman gave him a welcoming handshake and a greeting that only he was qualified to dare: "Hiya Gipper!"

No one at the Pentagon really expected the congresswomen to accept invitations for an overnight stay aboard the aircraft carrier Midway. It was shortly after World War 11 in a very masculine society. But Rep. Chase Woodhouse (D-Conn.) talked her colleague Rep. Reva Bosone (D-Utah) and a female press aide into daring to accept. Aboard the Midway, Adm. William Halsey greeted the women merrily. "I think you girls are great!" After watching planes land and take-off, the women retired to their private quarters, outside of which Halsey posted a guard. At dawn, Woodhouse asked whether the guard had been posted to protect the women or the crew. "You've got to know," said the much-decorated Halsey, "that you three are the first ladies who ever spent a night on the ship - legally."

Conditions at a hospital for the insane so appalled Rep. Al Vreeland (R-N.J.) that he helped the inmates though he didn't quite bargain for their kind of gratitude. Being a member of the District of Columbia Committee, Vreeland rammed through legislation making it more difficult to commit people to such hospitals. Appreciation was swift. Hordes of what he called "peculiar people on the borderline of insanity," turned up at his Capitol Hill office. One day he arrived to find his door barred by a rifle-toting man dressed as Daniel Boone, with fringed hunting jacket and burlap sacks for shoes. "Nobody goes in there to see that congressman until I say he can," the man growled. "Well, I am the congressman," said Vreeland. "Prove it!" the man barked. Vreeland had to comply before gaining entry.

*Young Rep. Everett Dirksen (R-Ill.) digressed from a debate to tell the story of a circuit court judge, with a fondness for corn liquor, who covered his Kentucky area on horseback. "Of course, he had to be circumspect about it so he put a bottle in his pocket and he had a rubber tube going up to his mouth. He could sit on the bench all day and puff vigorously but never any smoke curled from the bottle. But in the afternoon he would get what they call in Kentucky 'slightly mellow.' So this day he went out to throw the saddle on his horse. A young lawyer watching the operation noticed he had the pommel where the cantle should be. He said, 'Your Honor, you have got your saddle on backward.' Then, with that kind of dignity that only the judiciary can assume, he said, 'How in the devil do you know in what direction I am going?'"*

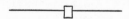

In her final campaign to round off 20 years in Congress, Edna Kelly (D-N.Y.) authorized her administrative assistant to spend $10,000 on stamps for her newsletter mailing. When she arrived in her New York office she almost keeled over in shock. Her assistant had spent all the money on stamps of Emmett Kelly the clown. The congresswoman quickly ordered them exchanged for something more appropriate.

*Freshman congressman John Allen (D-Miss.) won popularity across party lines for his unfailing wit and good humor. On his arrival in 1895 he quickly took note of everyone's titles and ranks and remarked, "In a House in which everybody is either a judge or a general, or a colonel, it is quite a distinction to be a private." Instantly, they nicknamed him Private John. When asked what his past conduct had been, Allen replied with good humor, "Never mind the past. I point with pride to my spotless future."*

When Rep. William Cole (R-N.Y.) became chairman of the Joint Committee on Atomic Energy in 1953 he decided to break years of secrecy and have open discussions on its peaceful uses. To safeguard national security, he allowed a classification officer from the Atomic Energy Commission to sit next to witnesses. If the officer stood up it would be a signal for Cole to drop the sensitive line of questioning. The officer stood up only once during the committee hearings. Cole pounded the gavel and demanded an explanation. "Never mind," said the officer as he flushed and sat down. Later, Cole cornered him. "What in the heck happened to you? Why did you stand up?" Replied the officer, "I only wanted to go to the bathroom."

*The employment agency sent a young girl to help with the overload of work in the office of Rep. Otha Wearin (D-Iowa). One day the congressman mentioned the word protocol during dictation. "What is protocol?" she asked. Wearin explained how it had to do with a person's standing in the political, economic and social sense. Still a bit puzzled, the stenographer asked, "Is a senator higher than a congressman?" Perhaps technically, said Wearin, because he would not think of leaving a social event before the senator. The stenographer thought for a moment then asked, "Is there anything lower than a congressman?" Replied Wearin: "If you read my mail long enough in this office you'll find out there probably isn't!"*

*The lives of congresswomen Emily Taft Douglas and Helen Gahagan Douglas seemed entwined like mating snakes. Both were theatrical stars of Broadway who had married in the same year. In 1944 both women won election as Democrats to the House of Representatives, Emily from Illinois and Helen from California, and they served together on the Foreign Affairs Committee. Their husbands had enlisted as privates during World War 11 and risen to the rank of major when, unknown to each other, they flew in to Washington from the South Pacific on the same day. Emily's husband, Paul - later elected to the Senate - arrived at the Capitol with his wounded arm in a plaster cast. He went up to the entrance of the House family gallery and told the usher he was Major Douglas just in from the South Pacific and wanted to see his wife. "Oh yeah," the usher mocked, "Major Douglas, just back from the South Pacific, is now in the gallery with his wife, congresswomen Douglas!" To Paul's surprise, it happened to be true. Major Melvyn Douglas, Helen's husband, had arrived a half hour earlier.*

**S**en. Theodore Green (D-R.I.) loved the social whirl in Washington. At one cocktail party he was asked how many he had attended that evening, "Four," Green replied as he pulled out a notebook from his pocket. "Are you trying to find out where you're going next?" the questioner asked. "No," said Green, "I'm trying to find out where I am now."

The House Ways and Means Committee was discussing investment tax credits with Secretary of the Treasury C. Douglas Dillon when the chairman asked Rep. Martha Griffiths if she had any questions. "Yes," said the Michigan Democrat who was the first female on the committee. "Gentlemen, be quiet," said the chairman. "For the first time in the history of the United States a woman will ask a question on this committee." Much later Dillon said her presence was the best thing that ever happened to the committee. Her interpretation was that the committee had been forced to clean up its language.

*T*hree months before his assassination in 1935, Sen. Huey "King-fish" Long (D-La.) filibustered against industrial legislation with a mix of impish gall and folksy chatter. For 16 hours his imaginative gibberish kept them laughing. "Speak loud enough for senators on the floor to hear and for the occupants of the gallery to hear," the vice president teased as he joined in the fun. A passing reference to Vincent Astor's $5 million yacht reminded Long that he had been governor when ships sailed into New Orleans during Prohibition. "I used to go on board foreign ships that came from countries where they manu-factured beer and articles of that kind in order to investigate and see if they were violating the law. And, I may say, that the laws were well enforced, in fact so well that when the Prohibition law was re-pealed nobody could tell the difference in that city."

Long kept his speech light and unpredictable. He jumped from reciting the biblical Book of Ecclesiastes to a tall story about a beloved uncle who took pity on a young bartender about to lose his job because he did not know how to mix drinks properly. "My uncle went down to the place where he was working one morning and put his foot on the rail and said to the young man, 'I am going to stay here with you until you find out how to mix drinks which the people like.' And my uncle stayed there with him all that day until closing time that night, and directed him how to mix the drinks, and drank them until he found out that the young man had mixed them right. He gave his time the whole day long to helping that young man. That is the kind of a reputation my family has."

Mischievously, Long gave recipes for celebrated Louisiana dishes, providing detailed instructions for the preparation of grease-fried salted oysters and potlikker soup made from turnips, greens and sliced side-meat. "Potlikker," he explained to raucous laughter, "is the residue that remains."

It was idle small talk until the committee staffer, a Harvard graduate, declared that while in the South he had dated a girl from Mississippi. "What was her last name," asked Rep. John Bell Williams of Mississippi. "Hayoud," said the staffer. "Hayoud? I thought I knew all of the Lebanese in Mississippi, but I don't believe I know them," said Williams. "She wasn't Lebanese," the staffer countered. "With a name like that she had to be," said Williams. "How do you spell it?" "H-E-A-D, but she pronounced it Hayoud," said the staffer, to the huge enjoyment of the southerner.

———————□———————

*When John Ingalls was president pro tem of the Senate he used an hour glass filled with sand to time the five minutes allowed for each speech. As soon as all the sand reached the bottom half the Kansas Republican promptly cut off a senator in mid-sentence. "It takes sand to run the Senate," he quipped.*

Lyndon Johnson's inexhaustible drive and energy hit top gear when he took over leadership of the Senate Democrats during the fifties. The towering Texan wielded much of his authority by exploiting an intimate knowledge of the strengths and weaknesses of his fellow senators. Every scrap of information was filtered into his memory to be used at the most opportune moment. When a new crop of Western senators was elected to Congress in a Democratic landslide, Johnson kept watchful tabs on them. The newcomers arrived in early December, hoping to tend to accommodation and other private matters before the January session got underway. Johnson gave them scant time to themselves. He called one meeting after another to learn more about their hopes and fears. After one such meeting, a freshmen senator asked an old-timer, "Why does Johnson hold these meetings? Does he work this way all the time? Doesn't he realize that Rome wasn't built in a day?" To which the veteran senator replied, "Yes, but Johnson wasn't the foreman of that job."

Humorist Mark Twain arrived in Washington to press for a new copyright bill but discovered the only people allowed to lobby on the floor of the House of Representatives were former congressmen and anyone "to whom the thanks of Congress had been extended." Immediately, he wrote a letter to the Speaker:

Lamb's Biographical Dictionary of the U.S.

*Mark Twain*

*Please get me the thanks of Congress - not next week, but right away! By persuasion if you can; by violence if you must ....... I have arguments with me - also a barrel with liquid in it ........ I have stayed away and let Congress alone for seventy-one years and am entitled to its thanks. Congress knows it perfectly well and I have long felt hurt that this quite proper and earned expression of gratitude has been merely felt by the House and never publicly uttered. Send me an order on the Sergeant-at-Arms quick! When shall I come?*

*-- With love and benediction,*
*Mark Twain*

When the House voted  $12,000 a year in support of a privately built library to house Franklin Delano Roosevelt's books and State papers at his Hyde Park, N.Y. retreat, Rep. Harold Knutson (R-Minn.) nearly choked. The papers, he suggested, should be brought to Washington, D.C. so that future statesmen might learn "how not to run a government."

*Despite Jean Terry's fear of flying she told her husband, Congressman John Terry (R-N.Y.), "The only time I'll fly is on Air Force One." Terry lightheartedly repeated this to his friend, Rep. Jack Kemp (R-N.Y.) and when both men were at a White House breakfast Kemp passed on the tale to President Nixon. When Terry got back to the Capitol a call came from the White House inviting him and his wife to fly with the president on Air Force One to Cape Canaveral. Terry thought it was a practical joke but after authenticating the call he got through to his wife, blurting, "You've been called!" Together they joined the president but when they arrived back in Washington Terry tried to make a reservation for his wife's flight home to New York. "I'll take the train," she insisted.*

A couple of senators once banded together to perk up a colleague's spirits with a little bit of "old-age humor." Sen. George Vest (D-Mo.) was in visibly frail health even though he was then only in his mid sixties. One day he looked particularly sad as he sat with his head in his hands in the Senate chamber. Sen. Shelby Cullom (R-Ill.) took pity on him and nudged Sen. Justin Morrill (R-Vt.), a Senate old-timer then in his mid eighties. "Why don't you go over and cheer up Vest?" Cullom suggested. Morrill thought it a good idea and shuffled over. "Vest, what's the matter?" he asked mischievously. "Cheer up! Why, you're nothing but a boy!" Vest had the last laugh. He outlived Morrill by six years.

———— ▯ ————

*Usher Burdick (R-N.D.) seldom rose to speak during debates in the House of Representatives. In mid-July 1951 he made a short speech. At the conclusion, as he prepared to sink back into quiet obscurity, he added a thoughtful line for all his colleagues: "I'd like to take this opportunity to wish you a Merry Christmas and a Happy New Year."*

*A late-night mix-up in a hotel room led to a warm friendship between two mainstays of the Senate. It took place in 1902 after Sen. Joseph Foraker (R-Ohio.) and Sen. George Hoar (R-Mass.) had uncharacteristically been at odds over legislation. Hoar's cordiality towards his fellow Republican turned ice-cold for the next three months. After Congress adjourned for the summer, Foraker stayed overnight in a New York hotel and went to bed early, forgetting to lock his door. A slight noise woke him up in the middle of the night. As he lay still he realized, to his horror, that a burglar was moving about. Suddenly the intruder switched on the light. Foraker did a double take. Instead of a burglar he saw the senator from Massachusetts. Sheepishly, Hoar explained how he had booked in at the hotel earlier that night and gone up to his room. A while later he had gone down to the lobby to mail a letter. On his return he had been surprised to find his light out. Only now did he realize that he had gotten out of the elevator a floor too soon. His room was another floor up, precisely above Foraker's. The two old men could not contain their guffaws. From then on they were friends again.*

———————□———————

A former radio announcer who won election to Congress upset the Speaker by secretly installing a deafening amplifying system in the House chamber in 1935. When Speaker Joe Byrns (D-Tenn.) gaveled for order the thump was amplified so loudly that he ordered the equipment removed. The culprit, Nebraska Republican Karl Stefan, said he had installed the system only on a trial basis. However, the amplifiers brought smirks to the faces of many members. They caught the distinctly private remarks of members seated unwittingly near the five microphones.

The way Sen. Mahlon Dickerson saw it there was no way Oregon could ever become a state and part of the Union. It was a mathematical absurdity. The New Jersey lawmaker tried to make this clear to fellow senators in 1825: "The whole distance from Washington ..... is 4650 miles. The distance, therefore, that a member of Congress of the state of Oregon would be obliged to travel to the seat of government and returning home, would be 9,300 miles ....... Every member of Congress ought to see his constituents once a year ...... If he should travel at the rate of 30 miles per day it would require 306 days. Allow for Sundays 44, it would amount to 350 days. This would allow the member a fortnight to rest himself at Washington, before he should commence his journey home."

CBS sprang a surprise on freshman Sen. Gale McGee (D-Wyo.) when he arrived in Washington to be sworn in. On the inaugural series called Meet The New Senators the interviewer suddenly approached McGee's parents, both staunch conservative Republicans from Nebraska. "Mrs. McGee," he said, "I've learned that you and Mr. McGee are Republicans. May I ask you just one question? What happened to Gale?" Without hesitation, she replied, "Well, we have often talked about it. We decided that we made our mistake when we sent him to college where he learned to read." The upshot was a flood of mail for the new senator in praise of his wonderful mother.

----------□----------

*One of the favorite jokes told by House Majority Leader Hale Boggs (D-La.) concerned identical and beautiful twin sisters who grew up in a small town. One of them married the local barber and after a while the other sister moved in with them. One day a customer asked the barber, "Charley, we just wonder about one thing. How do you tell them apart?" The barber didn't flinch. "Shucks," he said, "I don't try to tell them about it. I feel it's their responsibility."*

The filibuster had gone on for several straight nights when cots were brought in for Republican senators forced to stay put to keep the quorum. Sen. John Bricker (R-Ohio) leaned over to speak to Sen. William Jenner (R-Ind.) in the adjacent cot. "Bill, this is an awful way to serve your country, isn't it?" Replied Jenner: "Don't let my father find this out. When I became state chairman he thought I was getting along. When I was elected to the U.S. Senate he thought I had arrived. If he finds out I'm just nothing else but a night watchman he'll bring me home!"

Quick thinking saved Sen. William Proxmire some money and perhaps his life when two armed robbers accosted him in the nation's capital. "Go ahead and shoot. I have terminal cancer and I'll be dead in two weeks anyway," the Wisconsin Democrat hoodwinked. The thugs expressed sympathy by running off.

Sen. Alben Barkley loved a good joke, even if told at his own expense. The Kentucky Democrat used to tell of the gossip following the death of his first wife and his remarriage to a much younger woman. When asked how the marriage was going, Barkley said it was just fine. But didn't they ever argue? Not according to Barkley. "My wife and I had an agreement when we married that she would make all the small decisions and I would make all the big ones. So far, we haven't had any big decisions to make."

———————□———————

*John "Klu" Kluczynski was beloved by fellow congressmen for his abiding sense of humor. Long after his death in 1975 they were still dining out on Chicago-born Kluczynski's encounter at the White House with President Truman. Plain-speaking Truman had asked how everything was in Chicago. "Just the same," said Kluczynski. "What do you mean?" asked the president. "Well," Kluczynski explained, "the Polish get the votes and the Irish get the jobs!"*

A senator's whispered message was so inaudible that it led to a misunderstanding which brought howls of laughter from other lawmakers. When Anson McCook, secretary of the Senate, announced his impending marriage, senators decided to buy him a wedding gift. Sen. Jonathan Chace (R-R.I.) did the rounds asking for contributions. When he approached Sen. Joseph Dolph (R-Ore.) he spoke softly for fear McCook, the bridgroom-to-be, might overhear. Dolph expressed astonishment. He left the chamber and made straight for the cloakroom. "I have just had a request that beats any demand I have ever had made on my pocket-book," he told other senators gathered around. "Chace just came to me and in a mysterious way said that his cook was about to be married, and that he wanted to have me subscribe!" When the misunderstanding was pointed out, Dolph joined in the laughter.

*When his turn came to speak during the marathon debate on the Civil Rights Act of 1957, Sen. Allen Ellender (D-La,) couldn't resist a little dig at himself and other filibusterers, which brought laughs all round. "I held the title of the longest filibuster for about two or three years," he said, "until another idiot, in the person of the senior Senator from Oregon (Wayne Morse) beat my record."*

Augustus Hill had such a craving for candy that he brought packets of them into the Senate chamber and munched all through the debates in the late 19th century. The temptation to play a practical joke on the sweet-toothed Arkansas Democrat finally got the better of his colleagues. They coated small soap balls with sugar to resemble Hill's candies and slipped them into an open packet on his desk when he wasn't looking. All eyes were on him as he sat at his desk, absorbed in a book, and reached out for a candy. The foul taste soon showed on his expression. However, in attempting to preserve his dignity, Hill swallowed the soap ball instead of spitting it out. But his eyes began to water and as he looked up he saw the merry smiles on the culprits' faces. Hill took it all in good form and joked about it long after he became Attorney General.

When former House Speaker John Nance Garner was nominated as Franklin Roosevelt's running mate he gave a single campaign speech. Asked to explain, "Cactus Jack" told the story of a Texas ranger turning up to quell a riot. When asked by alarmed citizens why he had come alone, the ranger responded, "Just one riot ain't there!"

———————□———————

*New Jersey Republican congressmen William Widnall and Frank Osmers partied many a night together and used each other as excuses for being out late, each one saying he had been out with the other. After one heavy night ended in the wee hours of the morning, Widnall got in to his office nursing a bad hangover. Feeling sorry for himself he picked up the phone and called Osmers' office. "He's lying down on the couch," said the secretary. "That's fine, put him on," instructed Widnall. When Osmers came on Widnall asked, "Frank, what's the matter? Why are you lying down on the couch at this hour of the morning?" Osmers answered, "I just find I can tie a bow tie better this way."*

# LAST GASPS

— ▯ —

*The business of the Congress is tedious beyond expression*

*--John Adams*

When John Quincy Adams clutched at his desk and slumped over in the House of Representatives a cry went up from a legislator seated nearby: "Mr. Adams is dying!" The House hastily adjourned as congressmen rushed to bring in a sofa. Gently they lay the stricken former president of the U.S. across its length and carried him out into the Rotunda. Attending physicians suggested they carry the sofa with the 80-year-old Adams out the east portico

Lamb's Biographical Dictionary of the U.S.

*John Quincy Adams*

to give him fresh air but when they got there they decided it was too chilly. The Speaker of the House intervened, instructing them to move the couch, with Adams, to his official room.

Once there, the sixth president of the U.S. revived fleetingly and uttered his last words: "This is the end of earth but I am composed." When his English-born wife, Louisa, arrived, he gave no sign that he was aware of her presence and she bowed to the entreaties of physicians to leave the room. Adams, who remains the only man elected to the House of Representatives after a tenure as president, lay in a coma throughout the next day and well into the following evening. The man affectionately nicknamed "Old Man Eloquent" passed away amidst sorrow at 7:20 p.m. on February 23, 1848.

Both of Sen. Arthur Brown's previous wives had threatened to kill him but he was finally done in by a jilted mistress. Annie Bradley, a petite brunette in her mid-thirties, swore she "loved the ground he walked on" after plugging him with two bullets, one of which lodged in his pelvic area. Brown (R-Utah), was engaged to be married to yet another woman when he was slain in his Washington, D.C. hotel room. During the murder trial in 1907 female spectators outnumbered males in the packed courtroom. According to testimony Brown's first wife shot at him but missed after discovering his affair with the woman who became his second wife. When the second wife caught the senator with Annie Bradley in an Idaho hotel she put a choke-hold on the mistress. The senator parted the struggling women then promptly denied he was the father of his wife's son while confessing he had fathered his mistress's children. Annie Bradley divorced her own husband in the expectation of marrying the senator. But when Brown failed to follow through on his promise they, too, fought. She jabbed him in the mouth with he parasol, knocking out some of his teeth. Annie Bradley trailed the 63-year-old lawyer to Washington where he planned to argue a case before the supreme court. Just before she shot the former senator she asked if he would "do the right thing by me" and marry her. Brown's fatal reaction was to put on his overcoat and make for the door. "I shot him. I abhor acts of this character, but in this case it was fully justified," she told the court. The jury agreed. So did the spectators, who applauded her acquittal.

*Annie Bradley trailed the 63-year-old lawyer to Washington where he planned to argue a case before the supreme court. Just before she shot the former senator she asked if he would "do the right thing by me" and marry her. Brown's fatal reaction was to put on his overcoat and make for the door.*

*Rep. Preston Brooks (D-S.C.) died painfully after gaining notoriety for bludgeoning anti-slavery advocate Sen. Charles Sumner (R-Mass.) on the floor of the Senate. Confined to his bed at Brown's Hotel in Washington, Brooks was visited frequently by congressional colleagues who kept him up-to-date on legislative activity. One congressman was in the room when Brooks suddenly clutched his throat, gasping "Air! Air!" The congressman rushed to open a window, unaware that at that moment a doctor attending a patient in another room was on his way out and actually passed by Brook's closed door. In no time at all, Preston Brooks was dead.*

---

There was no hint of drama when Sen. Alben Barkley stood before 1700 students in a mock convention at Washington and Lee University to review his public service as congressman and vice president. But 15 minutes into his speech he said, "I would rather be a servant in the House of the Lord than sit in the seat of the mighty." They were the last words of the genial Kentucky Democrat who knocked over the microphone as he crashed to the floor, dead. His wife rushed to the stage from her front row seat but doctors said Barkley, who was Harry Truman's vice president, had died instantly of a heart attack.

*S en. Harry Lane (D-Ore.) may have lived a lot longer if he had not taken such a strong stand against American entry into World War 1. So many outraged voters in Oregon wanted him thrown out of Congress that Lane, 61, suffered a nervous breakdown and died two months later of a blood clot on the brain.*

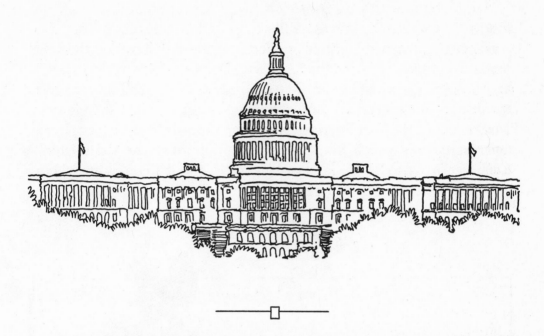

Born into slavery on a southern plantation, Jeremiah Haralson's triumphant election to Congress in1874 was overshadowed years later by the chilling news that wild animals had almost certainly made a meal of him. Haralson, then 70, met his reported grisly fate while mining coal in Colorado. A man with a stentorian voice and blazing eyes, he taught himself to read and write after the Civil War. Georgia-born, Haralson farmed before his elections to the Alabama state house and senate. He shunned the limelight during his single term in the House of Representatives, seldom speaking and taking a back seat rather than one offered him up front. A friend of Jefferson Davis, Haralson strived for better race relations, declaring "we must drive out these hell hounds and go in for peace between the two races in the South." Defeated in his relection bids, he moved from one state to another until his luck ran out in Colorado.

High drama struck the Senate chamber during a tedious debate on funding a communications satellite corporation. Sen. Estes Kefauver was speaking when he suddenly pulled up in agony. Observers thought it might be indigestion but the Tennessee Democrat was having a heart attack. Kefauver whispered to Sen. Frank Lausche (D-Ohio) to suggest the absence of a quorum. By not asking for the roll call himself, Kefauver would not lose the floor. He recovered his composure during the roll call and resumed his speech, though in obvious pain. When he had finished, Kefauver drove to Bethesda Naval Hospital, about 10 miles away, but was dead within a day and a half.

A split second decision to stand up proved fatal for Wisconsin Sen. Paul Hustings. In the moment that followed he was shot dead by his brother in a freak accident on Wisconsin's Rush Lake. They had been hunting ducks during a fall outing in 1917 when the first term Democrat spotted a flock. As he stooped low in his boat he called out to his brother in another boat to open fire. Brother Gustave obliged. Unfortunately, just as he squeezed the trigger his 51-year-old sibling stood up. The Senator was in the line of fire and took the shotgun blast to his back.

*Sam Houston*

$B$elieve it or not, though Sam Houston was born during George Washington's presidency, his son, Andrew, died an incumbent senator during World War 11. The 148-year span between the father's birth and the son's death was made possible because Sam was already 61 when Andrew was born. Sam's glorious exploits led to his becoming first president of the Republic of Texas, a U.S. Senator and then governor of Texas. Andrew, a West Point graduate and lawyer, was superintendant of the San Jacinto battleground, where his father won fame as victor over the Mexican General Santa Anna. When appointed to Congress in 1941 to serve until a special election filled the vacancy caused by the death of an incumbent, Andrew was, at 87, the oldest man ever to enter the Senate.

*Henry Wilson*

**R**umors that Vice President Henry Wilson was descended from gypsies were put to rest only after his fatal apoplectic attack in the Senate barber shop in 1875. Wilson, a former senator from Massachusetts, had rolled his head convulsively and though attendants rubbed his limbs with whiskey and salt he died in the Capitol 10 days later. After his funeral a surviving uncle and the Boston Herald  denied that his forebears were gypsies. They printed Wilson's genealogy, claiming that his great great grandparents, named Colbath, were immigrants from England and Ireland. The vice president was born a Colbath, but at age 21 he changed it to Wilson. His own explanation was that he was fascinated by the character and career of a contemporary by that name, General James Wilson, speaker of the New Hampshire House of Representatives.

*Sen. Richard Russell (D-Ga.) was only days away from death when an emissary from a Senate colleague arrived at his Washington, D.C. hospital room with an urgent appeal. Would Russell sign the prepared letter authorizing his proxy vote in favor of Sen. Robert Byrd (D-W.Va.) as majority whip? Every vote was crucial to Byrd in his uphill challenge to wrest the post from incumbent Sen. Edward Kennedy (D-Mass.). Byrd figured he could win by a single vote with Russell's backing. Russell, 73, agreed though he strained to complete his scrawled signature. On the day of the vote Byrd checked on the Georgian's health from dawn until the Democratic caucus met for the crucial mid-morning ballot. With seconds to go he learned Russell was still alive, which made his proxy vote valid. Byrd gave the nod for his name to be placed in nomination. To everyone's astonishment, Byrd won. Russell, however, never knew the result. The dean of the Senate had cast his final vote. He slipped into a coma and died four hours after Byrd's victory*

———————□———————

When Rep. Edward Eslick (D-Tenn.) dropped dead in the middle of a speech in 1932 it marked the first time a member had died on the floor of the House since completion of the Capitol almost a century before. Eslick, 60, championed bonus payments to veterans, and was in mid-sentence, declaring, "I want to go from the sordid side..." when he slumped forward. Witnesses in the packed galleries included his wife. The sudden drama caused such confusion that 40 minutes passed before the House adjourned.

———————□———————

# LEARNING THE ROPES

---□---

*We (the Senate) have the power to do any damn fool thing we want to do,
and we seem to do it about every 10 minutes.*

*-- Sen. William Fulbright (D-Ark.) 1952*

Freshman Rep. William Ayres thought it a great idea when a senior congressman suggested he write condolence letters to recently bereaved female constituents. Help offered with social security and other problems would pay dividends when he came up for reelection. So Ayres, (R-Ohio), looked through the obituary pages of the *Akron Beacon Journal* and churned out letters of sympathy. The practice came to an abrupt end with a tart reply from one widow. "Dear Congressman," she wrote, "I received your letter expressing sympathy regarding the passing of my late husband. If you had known how mean that SOB was to me you would have sent me a letter congratulating me on being rid of the bastard."

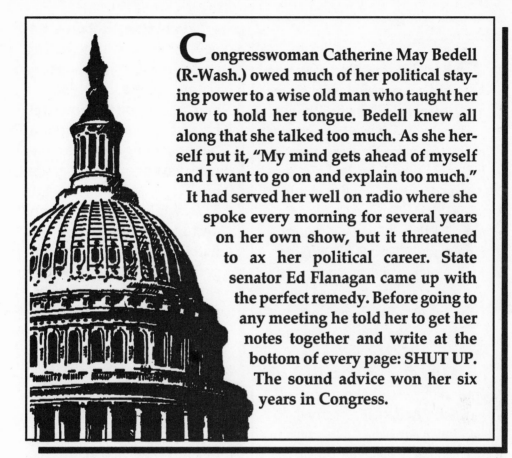

Congresswoman Catherine May Bedell (R-Wash.) owed much of her political staying power to a wise old man who taught her how to hold her tongue. Bedell knew all along that she talked too much. As she herself put it, "My mind gets ahead of myself and I want to go on and explain too much." It had served her well on radio where she spoke every morning for several years on her own show, but it threatened to ax her political career. State senator Ed Flanagan came up with the perfect remedy. Before going to any meeting he told her to get her notes together and write at the bottom of every page: SHUT UP. The sound advice won her six years in Congress.

Rep. Joseph Byrns, Jr. (D-Tenn.) rued the day he said he "wouldn't come home to shake hands with the clod-hoppers." It cost him the election in 1940. Clod-Hopper Clubs sprang up all over his district pledging support to the Independent candidate, J. Percy Priest, a folksy newspaper columnist born on April Fool's Day. As Priest stumped the district, fellow employees of his *Nashville Tennessean* pooled weekly small change to keep him on the payroll. Priest won the election, and the next seven as a Democrat. The clod-hopper's choice even became majority whip and chairman of the Committee on Interstate and Foreign Commerce.

*Fast-talking senators were the bane of Congressional Record reporters trying to keep up with every spoken word. Frank Attig, who reported for more than two decades before his retirement in 1974, was new on the job and more than jittery when his colleagues kept kidding him, "Wait until you get (Hubert) Humphrey!" For all his jovial nature, Humphrey was renowned as one of the fastest talkers on Capitol Hill. But Attig, a veteran court and legislative committee reporter, was more than his match. On the few occcasions Attig had to read back his transcript, Humphrey complimented, "Well, that's good reporting. Just what I said." Unknown to the popular Democrat, Attig had taken the tip of a more seasoned reporter, who counseled, "I've discovered a trick about Humphrey. He repeats himself. He's a fast talker, but he usually goes back and repeats something. In that way you can fill in what he said before if you didn't get it the first time."*

Republican Robert Denney hired a young man to stand outside a shopping center in Lincoln, Nebraska and take a poll on how well he was known to voters in the upcoming congressional race. He got only 3% against his Democratic opponent's 87% while 10% were undecided. Denney huddled with his brother and together they came up with a slogan, "Denney Will Win", to improve his chances. Sure enough, everywhere he went kids followed chanting, "Oh, no, Denney, you will not win." The general public began asking "Who's Denney? Why will he win?" Instantly, he had name recognition and won by a comfortable margin.

Speaker William Pennington was so ignorant of House rules and procedures that he did the bidding of a wise young page as if he were a ventriloquist's dummy. Pennington (Rep.- N.J.) had come to office in the 1850s as an unlikely compromise choice. He had scant knowledge of how to conduct business in the great chamber. By contrast, Morris was alert and wise to the ways of Congress. Inevitably, the old man leaned heavily on his knowledgeable page for guidance. But so complete was his obedience to the page that on one occasion he was left red-faced as he parrotted his instructions. Morris had dictated a course of action, closing with the words, "Now, go on!" Speaker Pennington dutifully did everything as instructed. But then, to Morris's astonishment, the Speaker ordered, "Now, go on!"

*When President Johnson agreed to make a reelection campaign appearance for Rep. Rodney Love (D-Ohio) an advance man gave the congressman a tip. "Remember, the president is coming to campaign for you. When you get off Air Force One do not let other dignitaries push you around, because they'll do it." Air Force One landed at Dayton and the president told the congressman, "When I get off the plane I want you right back of me." As they disembarked Sen. Frank Lausche (D-Ohio), the state governor and labor leader Walter Reuther all tried to push ahead, but the congressman blocked them. Seeing this, the president's advance man raised his hands above his head and flashed the V for victory sign.*

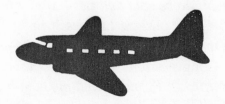

President Truman warned the future Queen of England to be prepared for "Fishbait" when she visited the House of Representatives. Otherwise known as William Mosley Miller, he was the diminutive House doorman, whose nickname derived from his puny size. "He's a real character," Truman jocularly told his royal visitor. "Fishbait" was scheduled to chaperone Princess Elizabeth and her husband, Prince Phillip, inside the House chamber, but the heir to the throne could hardly have been prepared for his informality. On her arrival he greeted her with a casual "Howdy, Ma'am." A startled State Department protocol officer quietly admonished Miller to "straighten up and fly right." But Mississippi-born "Fishbait" was unfazed by dignitaries. Standing on the rostrum with the princess, he called down to the floor, "Hey, pass me up the prince." Some years later the royal couple made a return visit, after Elizabeth had been crowned Queen, and she was accompanied by her own towering security guards. As "Fishbait" locked his hand on the Queen's elbow to help her up to the rostrum, one of the security guards struck the Mississippian's arm with the force of a karate chop, admonishing, "Commoners don't touch the Queen!" Reeling from the force of the blow, "Fishbait" never again touched British royalty.

*The first native of Asia elected to the U.S. Congress took the advice of veteran legislators, vowing to be seen and not heard. After his 1956 victory, Dalip Singh Saund (D-Calif.) pledged to himself to let Dwight Eisenhower remain president and Sam Rayburn continue as House Speaker. Poking fun at himself in his memoirs,* Congressman from India, *he wrote, "It was perhaps the wisest decision I ever made. I would mind my own business. I was going to attend to my job." It paid off for the immigrant lawyer. He was reelected.*

Rep. Gerald Ford (R-Mich.) almost blew his chances of election as House minority leader because his wife expected him home to charcoal steaks. During the 1965 strategy session in his Capitol Hill office, supporters pressed him to stay on and make 15 to 20 critical telephone calls. Rep. Charles Goodell (R-N.Y.) insisted, "Jerry, you're not going home to charcoal steaks now. You've got to make these calls. They want to know what you have in mind if you're going to be minority leader." Ford picked up the telephone to call home. "Geez," he said, "I don't know what Betty is going to say about this." Goodell thought Betty gave Ford a little bit of a hard time but the candidate didn't go home. He won the election and aides later confirmed that Ford's calls had indeed swung the vote his way.

When Iowa's Guy Gillette was elected to the Senate he let an old hand from the opposition pick the right moment for his maiden speech. Gillette, along with many others returned in the Democratic landslide, found the only seats available were across the aisle on the Republican side. He took a desk behind Hiram Johnson (R-Calif.). One day, Gillette came in armed with copious notes, obviously prepared to make his maiden speech. Johnson turned around and cautioned, "Senator, this is not the time. I'll tell you when to speak." Though taken aback, Gillette deferred to Johnson's experience. Some weeks later when a bill came up dealing with farmers, Johnson told the newcomer, "This is the one you speak on. This will be your maiden speech." Gillette agreed, considering he came from an agricultural state, and rose to speak for the first time.

———□———

*Rep. Marguerite Church (R-Ill.) learned within five days of her appointment to the Foreign Affairs Committee that travel abroad was more important than gladhanding voters from her district. When told that she had to leave instantly for India, Church huffed, "I can't go. I have some of the most important people in my district coming to Washington next week to see the sights and wherever else they expect to find me is not on the banks of the Sutlij River." She quickly regretted her stance. When Congress debated hostilities between India and Pakistan no one wanted to hear her opinions because she had not been there.*

A populist in public, Sen. Jeff Davis (D-Ark.) would often attack big business and plutocrats. In private, he was far more level-headed and even apologetic. One day he rose in the Senate to denounce Sen. Chauncey Depew (R-N.Y.) for his close ties to bankers, railroad barons and New York capitalists. When another senator whispered that he had gone too far because Depew could make a dangerous enemy, Davis went over to apologize. "I thought that you would not care," Davis told Depew, "because it won't hurt you and it does help me out in Arkansas." Depew shrugged it off, saying "Jeff, old man, if it helps you, do it as often as you like." But Davis got the message. He never again singled out Depew as a populist target.

**A** Republican member of the House was giving his party whip, Rep. Leslie Arends a hard time, declaring he would definitely vote against a bill that the GOP wanted to enact. Worse still, the out-of-line representative was beginning to influence other congressmen. Arends (R-Ill.) decided to turn the screws. He got the Republican president to invite the man to a White House breakfast. Backed by the enormous prestige of the highest office in the land, the chief executive applied overwhelming pressure, outlining exactly why he wanted the bill passed. The congressman soon knuckled under, explaining, "I played a lot of football when I was in college and I learned some things.  In football I never tackled my own quarterback. Mr. President, I won't tackle my own quarterback. I'll vote for the bill."

Julia Hansen's distinction in being the first woman to chair a House Appropriations subcommittee caused quite a flutter in 1967. Ill at ease, the committee chairman went the rounds asking whether she was good enough. He quit niggling after Hansen (D-Wash.) questioned whether he had given the same treatment to males. Hansen's own game plan to avoid a licking was to master parliamentary procedure. If she lost a fight she vowed never to whine, get mad or cry. When she handled her first bill Hansen got the ultimate compliment from the House parliamentarian. "Julia," he said, "I'm going to quit worrying about you."

*The best advice Ray Madden got during 34 years in Congress was from a man who'd served much longer than him, Rep. Adolph Sabath (D-Ill.). "Talk to the young people. They keep growing older and they all vote in a few years." Madden (D-Ind.) did just that and towards the end of his congressional career, a man came up to him at a county fair in his district. The stranger introduced his wife and adult son and daughter. "We first met in your second term when I was a junior at Horace Mann high school," the stranger told Madden. "You came out and talked to us. I got acquainted with you. I and my family voted for you ever since - although our family's always been Republican!"*

New Hampshire's Sen. Edward Rollins panicked every time he had to line up his Republican colleagues for an important vote. To make sure all GOP senators were present, Rollins, chairman of the Committee on Enrolled Bills, harassed veterans of the Senate staff as well as cowering pages to hunt down missing lawmakers. The pressure on them mounted amid much grumbling. After Rollins cracked the whip for yet another vote, the young pages decided to get their own back. The opportunity came when Rollins announced he was off to the restaurant. They waited until he was comfortably seated then all the pages appeared simultaneously and hollered in unison, "Voting, senator! Voting!" Rollins got the message.

When Congress was little more than a century old, Richard Bartholdt (R-Mo.) was sharply rebuffed by his colleagues when he tried to get the words *In God We Trust* removed from all U.S. coins. Though he believed in God he said religion had no place in politics. Besides, Bartholdt thought the words took the Lord's name in vain. But the subject proved too touchy for most congressmen. Even though many privately sided with Bartholdt, they voted against him because they did not want their constituents to think they were in any way anti-religious.

Sen. Robert Kerr (R-Okla.) never forgot the day freshman Sen. Wallace Bennett (R-Utah) saved him from public humiliation. It happened during debate on accelerated depreciation, which Kerr wanted to do away with. When Bennett got up to argue, Kerr scornfully told him to go and telephone the IRS to learn about it. Bennett, a former president of the National Association of Manufacturers, was very familiar with the provision. He challenged Kerr to make the same call. Kerr complied and a few minutes later skulked into the chamber. "You're not going to make me get up and admit I was wrong, are you?" he asked. "No, Bob," replied Bennett. From that day on Kerr gave favorable treatment to Bennett. And shortly before he died, Kerr sent out several personal messages of friendship. Among those remembered was Wallace Bennett.

*Davey Crockett*

**D**avey Crockett was a battlefield veteran and self-described "backwoodsman" who wanted none of the foppishness of the West Point Military Academy. After his election to the House of Representatives from Tennessee he called for closure of the prestigious Academy, claiming it educated the children of aristocratic and wealthy families at the expense of the poor. "The young men educated there do not suit our service," he told legislators in an impassioned speech in 1830. "They are too delicate and cannot rough it in the army. When they leave the school they are too nice for hard service." Crockett, who fell six years later in defense of the Alamo, knew the odds were stacked against him, noting, "There are too many gentlemen in the House interested in this Academy to allow the resolution to pass." An overwhelming majority of members proved him right on the last point.

Karl Mundt refused to quit the Senate after being hit by a crippling stroke. Sometimes the South Dakota Republican voted by proxy. However, for more than two years he absented himself from the Senate chamber and from the less glamorous but more important committee rooms. By 1972 Senate Republicans could no longer stomach it. Even though Mundt was highly respected and a national figure who chaired the McCarthy-Army hearings, his colleagues went further than they had ever gone before in yanking away rights of seniority. They stripped Mundt of his position as ranking Republican on the Government Operations Committee and as second-ranking minority member of the Foreign Relations and Appropriations Committees. The four-term Senator did not run for re-election that year. Two years later he was dead.

———————— ▯ ————————

Walter Judd (R-Minn.) had to admit after 20 years in the House of Representatives that Democrats were better party loyalists than Republicans. For proof he cited the race between Lyndon Johnson and John Kennedy for their party's presidential nomination. Judd was in an elevator with Johnson when the Texan wisecracked, "Have you heard the news? Jack's pediatricians have just given him a clean bill of health!" Judd was shocked by the insulting remark. But then Kennedy won and LBJ agreed to be his running mate - all in the interests of securing an election win for the party.

**Edited excerpts from a Senate debate, March 14, 1925:**

*Sen. Richard Ernst (R-Ky.):* I wish to know if there be any way under the rules of the Senate whereby I can, without breaking those rules and without offending the senators about me, call a fellow member a willful, malicious, wicked liar? Is there any way of doing that?

*Sen. Joseph Robinson (D-Ark.):* Every senator owes it to the body to which he belongs to prevent outrages upon the feelings of other senators and to protect the good name of the Senate itself from such conduct as the senator from Kentucky has just indulged in.

*Sen. James Watson (R-Ind.):* I hope my good friend from Kentucky will not make the charge that he was about to make.

*Sen. William Borah (R-Idaho):* It is a pathetic thing, a very pitiable thing, that we have reached a point here in the Senate of the United States where we cannot discuss public questions without indulging in personalities.

*Sen. James Heflin (D-Ala.):* I make the point of order that the senator from Virginia was addressing the Senate, and the senator from Kentucky was not recognized or yielded to by him to inject into the debate what he did. The senator from Virginia was taken off his feet by the occurrence; and if that is permitted to be done, all that a senator has to do to get the floor is to insult some other senator.

*The Presiding Officer, Sen. Simeon Fess:* The Chair must declare the point of order not sustained.

*Sen. Ernst:* I realize that the language I used was harsh. I desire to withdraw that parliamentary inquiry.....

# POLITICAL FLAIR

—————[]—————

*Some congressmen keep their ear so close to the ground that they get both ears on the ground. Only two other animals can do that · a donkey and a jack rabbit.*

*-- House Speaker Joe Cannon*

Henry Clay was much more than an outstanding House Speaker and senator. The Kentuckian was one of the best story-tellers in Congress. One of his favorites involved his role in negotiating the Treaty of Ghent which ended the war between the U.S. and Britain in 1814. While in Europe he wrote letters to his home state to be read aloud in public. A farmer was puzzled by frequent use of the words sine qua non. He interrupted the local politician reading the letter and asked for an explanation. Though just as ignorant, the quick-thinking politico replied, "Sine qua non is an island in Passamaquoddy Bay, and Henry Clay goes for Sine qua non!" The audience loved it and hooted approval for Clay's patriotism.

*Henry Clay*

Members of the Edgefield, S.C. ladies garden club scattered when a snake fell out of a tree at their open-air meeting but Congressman William Dorn kept his composure. His parents had trained him from fifth grade how to handle distractions during speeches. They used to have him memorize famous orations then recite them above the racket of giggling onlookers. Dorn (D-S.C.) became so polished that he won the medal every year at his school's declamation contest. By the time the snake dropped from the tree, Dorn had already won his political spurs by talking on as firecrackers exploded and trains sped by.

*Rep. Frank Becker (R-N.Y.) always had a trump card in explaining how he could vote against the wishes of most of his constituents. He used it to good effect in surviving five reelections through 1965. The source of his confidence was an 18th century British politician, Edmund Burke. The New Yorker made sure voters back home got printouts of Burke's wisdom. Sure, Burke had urged politicians to work closely with constituents. But the blunter part of Burke's quote was addressed to voters: "Your representative owes you not his conscience but his judgment. And he betrays, instead of serving you, if he sacrifices it to your opinion."*

*The high school principal put the senator on the spot by citing him as an alumnus, a graduate and a role model for the current graduating class. The trouble was, Sen. John Williams (R-Del.) had dropped out after 11th grade and never graduated. "How do I straighten it out?" wailed the principal. Williams knew how to handle it and agreed to speak. He told the students he deserved a thrashing for not graduating. However, he said the level of competition had been low when he was an adolescent. Most of his peer group had no more education than he did. By contrast, today's graduates had to go on to college because that was the level of contemporary competition.*

Florida Democrat Claude Pepper was the envy of many a congressman because his polished speeches were delivered after only scant preparation and without notes. His performances were acclaimed in the Senate and then in the House, where he sat for many years after losing a reelection bid to the Senate. Foreign Relations Committee chief of staff Francis Wilcox was in the Senate chamber one day when Pepper came in and asked what they were debating. Wilcox gave a hurried rundown on the accession of the U.S. to the Statute of the International Court of Justice. A short while later Pepper rose to speak on the issue. He was so good that the following day a State Department expert contacted Wilcox. "Gee, that was a great speech," he said. "Did you write it for him?" When told that Pepper's briefing had lasted no more than a few minutes, the expert was almost speechless.

Fed up with World War 11 austerity measures, the female constituent wrote Rep. George Outland (D-Calif.) that unless sliced bread was restored to the grocery shelves she would vote against him in the next election. Her letter arrived the same morning the congressman received a press release from the War Production Board announcing the ban on sliced bread would be lifted the following day. Hastily, Outland wrote the constituent: "I have taken the matter up personally with President Roosevelt and we have decided to restore sliced bread to the American people tomorrow." The voter replied forthwith. "Anybody who can go directly to the president and get as prompt and successful action on the request of a constituent is going to have my vote and that of all my relatives as long as you want to run for office."

Lyndon Johnson's skills as a political pro were never more obvious than in the way he eased doddering Sen. Theodore Green (D-R.I.) out of the chairmanship of the Foreign Relations Committee. Everyone but Green, 94, realized his memory was not what it used to be. He was also going blind and deaf. When the press called for him to step down he finally told Majority Leader Johnson (D-Tex.) that he planned to quit. Johnson assembled the entire committee and led off in pleading with Green to change his mind. "Theodore, you can't do this," he said with mock alarm. "You're the greatest chairman the committee has ever had." Other senators took up the same theme. They were so persuasive that Green began to have second thoughts. Johnson moved swiftly. Putting his arm around the old man, he coaxed, "Theodore, I wish you'd go outside and think about it a little bit. It's a very important decision you're making." Johnson ordered staff director Carl Marcy to accompany Green. Marcy guessed Johnon's intentions and told Green bluntly that he ought to stick with his resignation. Meanwhile, Johnson told the remaining senators that Green was sick and tired and that if he did not step down "he may not be with us for very long." When Green came back in to announce his resignation, Johnson proposed making him chairman emeritus. Everyone approved. Then Johnson turned to the ranking Democrat, Sen. William Fulbright of Arkansas and said, "Bill, you're the chairman." That done, he closed the meeting.

> *"Theodore, you can't do this," he said with mock alarm. "You're the greatest chairman the committee has ever had."*

**R**ep. Marguerite Church (R-Ill.) always believed she was "a little bit of a burden" to her male colleagues during the decade she traveled with them to the Far East as a member of the Foreign Affairs Committee. Her secret for winning their acceptance in the masculine-dominated 1950s turned on three rules she set for herself. She never complained. She never made a suggestion. She never came down to breakfast. "They could have that time to themselves!" she laughed.

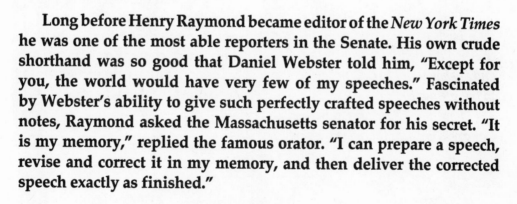

Long before Henry Raymond became editor of the *New York Times* he was one of the most able reporters in the Senate. His own crude shorthand was so good that Daniel Webster told him, "Except for you, the world would have very few of my speeches." Fascinated by Webster's ability to give such perfectly crafted speeches without notes, Raymond asked the Massachusetts senator for his secret. "It is my memory," replied the famous orator. "I can prepare a speech, revise and correct it in my memory, and then deliver the corrected speech exactly as finished."

*Henry Clay knew his fellow Kentuckians as well as they knew their hunting rifles. It paid off when it seemed they might not return him to Congress. Their anger followed his vote in favor of senators receiving an annual salary of $1500 to replace the per diem pay. "Fellow Kentuckians," he pleaded, "If you had a favorite rifle that had never missed fire, and one day that trusty old rifle should accidentally miss its mark, would you cast it away?"*

*"No! No!" they chorused.*

*"Would you not try it again?"*

*"Yes! Yes!" they responded.*

*"Then, fellow citizens, I am that trusty old rifle that never missed fire, and I ask you not to cast me aside, but to try me again."*

*They did. Clay was returned to Congress with an increased majority.*

**H**ouse Armed Services Committee chairman Carl Vinson (D-Ga.) had a reputation for being able to make a 180 degree turn on political issues. Vinson used to say, "When you start down a road, be sure to leave yourself room enough to turn around." At other times he would explain, "Well, I marched up the hill. Now I'm marching back down!" According to his fellow Georgian, Phillip Landrum, Vinson was "the nearest thing to a total legislator I've ever seen. If he saw he couldn't get through that window, he'd turn and come through this window. But in doing so, he never lost sight of where he was ultimately going."

Rep. William Lattimore felt so good about America that in 1805 he dashed off a letter to his constituents in the then Mississippi Territory: "Enjoying peace at home, respected abroad, possessing an annually increasing revenue, rich in vast territories for the setttlement of a fast growing population, and, above all, blest with genuine liberty, both civil and religious, what nation is so happy? Who is not thankful that he is an American? Who is not content with a government, created by the will, and devoted to the interests of the people?

Sen. Hiram Fong ( R-Hawaii) knew how to make the front page back home - even on a slow news day. One weekend as he sat outside the Senate chamber reading a newspaper, Capt. Leonard Ballard of the Capitol Police teased him. Pointing up to the light fixture shaped like a pineapple, Ballard said, "Well, Senator, our forefathers were pretty farsighted, weren't they? When they built this wing of the Capitol in 1857 they knew Hawaii would eventually be a state because they put a pineapple up here." Fong looked up astonished. He had never noticed it before. He raced off and came back shortly with an official photographer and two pineapples. Soon Fong had commandeered a 6 ft. ladder and clambered up, posing with his pineapples next to the unique light fixture. Pleased with himself when it was all over, Fong gave one of the pineapples to Ballard. Days later the captain received another gift from the senator. It was a clipping from the *Honolulu Bulletin*. Fong had made the front page with his picture and story.

*John F. Kennedy (D-Mass.) often sat down beside Judge Reva Bosone (D-Utah) in the House of Representatives and the two became good friends. She smiled when Kennedy pulled paperbacks out of his pocket during boring speeches. Years later, after Kennedy won the presidential election, he delivered the State of the Union address to Congress. Bosone slipped down the back stairs hoping to avoid the crowds. Others had the same idea but police stopped them all to make way for the president. Bosone was startled to hear her name. "Hello there, Judge Bosone!" said Kennedy as he reached over others to shake her hand. Bosone never forgot the smile on First Lady Jacqueline Kennedy's face. The two women had not met but Bosone thought "you could tell she was thinking that must be some old friend of Jack's the way that he did that thing."*

# FEARSOME & VIOLENT

—⊡—

*I attended (the Senate) a few times to hear the debates but was*
*unable to hear, at least distinctly, owing to the noise made in the galleries,*
*lobbies and that made by the slamming of the doors.*
*I was greatly surprised that so little order was maintained.*


*-- Anne Royall*
*Sketches of History, Life & Manners in the United States, 1826*

Simmering bitterness between two middle-aged congressmen from Missouri ended in a punch-up on Capitol Hill with the loser being treated for a cut lip and bruised eye. The 1933 fist-fight involved Rep. Clarence Cannon, 53, a former lawyer, history professor and author of several books on procedure in the House of Representatives. The man he got the better of was Rep. Milton Romjue, 58, a former judge of probate court. The two Democrats were pulled apart by a passing Minnesota congressman who shoved one of the Missourians into an elevator in the old House Office Building.

Pamela Young left for an extended stay in South America convinced that her Washington, D.C. furnished apartment was in good hands because she had sub-let to a congressman. But she knew nothing about Marion Zioncheck's drunken orgies and bizarre conduct. She raced back to the nation's capital when she heard he had smashed her possessions and damaged her home, assaulted a policeman and, on New Year's Day 1936, tied up a telephone operator and roused dozens of sleeping residents to convey season's greetings. Young, a widow, quickly repossessed her home while the 34-year-old congressman was away on his honeymoon. However, when Zioncheck (D-Wash.) returned, he evicted her so forcefully that she was hospitalized with multiple bruises and suspected fractures. When Young tried again to reclaim her home Zioncheck grabbed her legs, the congressman's wife seized her head and arms and together they dumped the unfortunate woman in the corridor.

Zioncheck was taken for observation to a hospital after delivering empty beer bottles to the White House and driving his car up the sidewalk on the wrong side of the road. Transferred by his wife to a private sanitarium to evade arrest on charges of assaulting Young, the freshman representative escaped to his Capitol Hill office. On the intervention of the House sergeant-at-arms, Zioncheck, a lawyer, received safe passage back to Seattle. There the congressman campaigned for reelection until committing suicide by leaping from his fifth-floor office window onto his car.

*John Randolph of Roanoke*

John Randolph of Roanoke normally subdued his enemies with a withering lash of his tongue but the spindly Virginian did not hesitate to tangle physically. While he was House Republican leader in 1804 he took an intense dislike to Rep. Willis Alston. One night they exchanged heated words across the dinner table at a Washington boarding house. As soon as the female diners left the room the aristocratic Randolph poured himself a glass of wine, splashed it in Alston's face and broke the glass over his antagonist's head. Alston retaliated by hurling a decanter. After throwing tableware at each other, Randolph scornfully retired to his quarters.

Six years passed before they clashed again. When the House adjourned on a motion by Randolph, Alston remarked loudly, "the puppy still has respect shown him!" Randolph caught up with Alston on the stairs and roared, "I have a great mind to cane him, and I believe I will!" He knocked Alston's hat off and pounded him so severely that he drew blood. Alston kicked and swore, trying all the while to lunge at Randolph's throat before other congressmen parted the two. The next day Alston appeared in the House with a bandaged head. A local court fined Randolph $20 for causing a breach of the peace. It was, commented one wit, a fair valuation of Alston's head.

Two 61-year-old senators shocked onlookers as they wrestled wildly on the floor of the Capitol in 1964. It began playfully when Ralph Yarborough (D-Tex.) tried to pull Strom Thurmond (D-S.C.) into the Commerce Committee room to make up a quorum. By staying put outside, Thurmond hoped to block approval of a presidential nominee to a civil rights position. As Yarborough grabbed Thurmond's sleeve and light-heartedly pulled him towards the room the South Carolinian said, "I'll make an agreement with you, Ralph. If I can keep you out, you won't go in. And if you can drag me in, I'll stay there." In a flash the scuffle became a brawl as Thurmond, 170 pounds, pinned the 200-pound Texan to the floor. During the fracas a horrified colleague warned them to quit before they both had heart attacks. Thurmond taunted, "Tell me to release you, Ralph, and I will." The Texan struggled to his feet but was floored again as the locked senators swayed back and forth along the ornate corridor. Alerted by the ruckus, Commerce Committee chairman Warren Magnuson (D-Wash.) demanded an end to the undignified free-for-all. "Come on, you fellows, let's break this up!" They relaxed their holds, brushed themselves off and slipped into the committee room. With the nominee approved over Thurmond's sole objection the two senators went their ways apparently the best of friends. "It was all in jest," Thurmond explained. Yarborough said his own weight advantage had not been enough to overcome Thurmond's benefit of "guerilla training at Fort Bragg."

Less than nine years after the opening of the first Congress, two men brawled savagely with canes and fire tongs on the floor of the House of Representatives. In January 1798, Roger Griswold of Connecticut overheard Matthew Lyon of Vermont sneeringly remark that he might go to Connecticut to publish a paper in a fight for democracy. Griswold, 36, taunted, "When you come over to Connecticut to fight for democracy, are you going to wear your wooden sword?" Enraged, Lyon, 48, spit tobacco juice in Griswold's face. After a motion to expel Lyon "for a violent attack and gross indecency" failed, Griswold waited a few weeks before taking revenge.

Immediately after House morning prayers, as Lyon sat at his desk, Griswold approached shouting "rascal!" and struck him fiercely on the head and shoulders with a large yellow hickory cane. Lyon fled to the fireplace behind the Speaker's chair, seized the fire tongs and turned on Griswold. The two flailing congressmen fell to the floor. They were dragged apart by members seizing hold of Griswold's legs even as the Speaker stood nearby reprimanding, "That is not a proper way to take hold of him. You ought to take hold of him by the shoulders." Lyon, sporting a black eye, limped off to a shelf to drink some water but when he found himself standing next to Griswold he struck him with a cane. Another member rushed in to arm Griswold with a cane of his own as Lyon challenged, "Come on!" Several congressmen pushed themselves between the belligerents and when the Speaker called for order even Griswold took his seat. Six days later the House voted down motions to expel or censure both Griswold and Lyon.

*Matthew Lyon, (left) battles Roger Griswold in the House of Representatives, 1798*

After *Louisville Times* reporter Charles Kincaid shot dead a former congressman in the U.S. Capitol a jury acquitted him of murder, a judge set him free and court spectators had to be restrained from cheering. The bloody incident began in 1888 when congressman William Taulbee (D-Ky.), noted for his bullying ways and loud voice, reportedly had an affair with a female working in the Patent Office. When Kincaid wrote follow-ups on published accounts of the scandal, the tall, physically powerful Taulbee saw red. For more than a year he hounded the 5 ft. 3 in. newsman with verbal abuse and threats of violence. During a brief encounter in the Capitol in the winter of 1890 Taulbee tweaked the reporter's ear, warning he had better arm himself. Kincaid took his tormentor's advice. Less than two hours later the two Kentuckians clashed on a staircase leading to the Capitol basement. Kincaid fired a single revolver shot into Taulbee's head. The tough ex-congressman, who had represented a mountain district, held out for 11 days of noisy delirium before dying.

W*hen Sen. Joe McCarthy kicked syndicated columnist Drew Pearson in the groin, then Sen. Richard Nixon quickly parted the two to save the newsman from possibly being killed. The flare-up climaxed a running feud between the Wisconsin Republican, then at the height of his campaign to smear innocents with the communist tag, and the celebrity newsman who sought to expose him. McCarthy had threatened physical harm to Pearson before kneeing and punching him in the coat-check room at Washington's exclusive Sulgrave Club on Pearson's 53rd birthday. Nixon said later that if he hadn't stepped in to pull off McCarthy, the enraged senator "might have killed Pearson." As for the winded Pearson, he left the Club keeping a watchful lookout for McCarthy.*

It was best to steer clear of the elevator when Sen. Boies Penrose was around. This was where the 6 ft. 4 in. Pennsylvania Republican, who weighed close to 400 lbs., often let loose with his fearsome temper. A power broker within his party, he looked and behaved like a Prussian guardsman in his contempt for the common man. One day, as he got into the elevator to go up to the Senate chamber, a chirpy elevator boy said, "Good morning, senator." Penrose replied tartly, "I don't speak to hired help." A few days later, when the elevator operator repeated his greeting, the senator snapped, "I told you once, I don't speak to hired help!" To prove his clout, Penrose had the boy removed from the payroll within an hour. Another time he shook the bars of the elevator cage violently as he waited impatiently for its arrival. And when a male member of the public innocently blocked the senator's path, Penrose picked him up and dumped him on the side before boarding the elevator.

*Boies Penrose*

No authority in the House of Representatives had dared challenge the theatrical conduct of arrogant John Randolph of Roanoke. After early morning horse rides hunting quail, the eccentric Randolph swaggered into the House, booted, spurred and clutching a riding whip. One or two of his hunting dogs followed, sniffing congressmen and occasionally barking during speeches. When Kentucky's Henry Clay banished the dogs from the chamber after becoming Speaker in 1811 the lines were drawn. Their feud intensified over war with Britain, which Clay championed and Randolph opposed.

In 1826 they dueled with pistols after Randolph mocked President John Quincy Adams's alliance with Clay as a combination "of the puritan with the blackleg." Both men missed their first shots. Clay's second attempt struck on target but could not penetrate the layers of coats. Randolph aimed his final shot skywards and approached his adversary with an outstretched hand. "You owe me a coat, Mr. Clay," said Randolph. "I am glad the debt is no greater," Clay replied.

———————□———————

**Wealthy farmer and representative Fred Crawford, 61, slugged one of his congressional aides then wound up in jail for two nights on a matter of principle. The nine term Michigan Republican had offered cash or securities for bail on the assault charge but was told he could only put up a real estate bond or go through a professional bondsmen. When authorities relented, he chose jail, arguing that congressmen should not be given favors denied other citizens. Crawford received a $25 fine for punching his male assistant in the 1950 dispute involving the congressman's stenographer. Back in the House of Representatives, he got a standing ovation for refusing the offer of special privileges.**

In the mid-19th century Congressman Philemon Herbert shot dead a waiter who refused to bring him breakfast at the Willard, Washington's most exclusive hotel. Bedlam broke out shortly after Herbert (D-Calif.) sat down at a dining-room table with his roommate, William Gardiner. Hotel policy was not to serve breakfast after 11 a.m. without the approval of management. At the murder trial, waiters denied Herbert's claim that he made the deadline. One hotel servant said he heard the Alabama-born congressman call the young married waiter, Thomas Keating, "a damned Irish son-of-a-bitch!" Enraged, Keating reached for a plate while the 30-year-old representative grabbed a chair. Within seconds crockery, glasses and a silver salver were used as weapons. Half a dozen waiters joined in the fray, hurling tableware and bloodying Herbert's nose.

The commotion brought Keating's brother, Patrick, rushing in from the kitchen. On seeing the congressman with a pistol in one hand and a chair in the other, Patrick seized a pitcher of molasses and a sugar bowl and plowed into the melee. The containers broke and molasses spilled over several combatants. Herbert's friend, who testified that it was the waiter who had provoked the congressman, picked up a chair and smashed it down so hard against the waiters that it broke. The French cook, Devenois, eating breakfast in the kitchen, did not pause at the sound of falling china because "plates and glasses were always being broken." But at the sound of a shot the chef ran to the dining room and saw Thomas Keating clutching his breast. As the wounded waiter pulled his hands

- continued -

*away blood gushed out. "Sauvez-vous!" (save yourself!) the cook screamed at Patrick, urging him to flee. Women gathered by the dining room entrance shrieked at the bloody spectacle. A Dutch diplomat who later refused to testify, sat composed throughout, enquiring only at the end of the fracas whether Keating was dead.*

*At the four-day trial, a defense witness said he had seen four or five servants "breaking plates upon Herbert's head as fast as they could make the licks." The prosecutor regretted that times had changed so much since the last presidential election "when the sweet Irish brogue and German accent were so much courted." Herbert's attorneys, pleading self-defense, decried attempts to politicize the trial and portray it as a class war between the haves and have-nots. When the not guilty verdict was announced the overflow crowd cheered loudly.*

*Lambasted as a beast and murderer by the* San Francisco Evening Bulletin, *Herbert did not run for reelection. He moved to Texas and in1864 died of wounds sustained while a Confederate officer at the battle of Mansfield.*

SCENE IN UNCLE SAM'S SENATE.
17? APRIL 1850

The years before the Civil War witnessed tumultuous debates in the Senate over slavery. In 1850 Thomas Benton of Missouri and Henry Foote of Mississippi came close to killing or seriously injuring one another on the floor of the chamber. Pandemonium broke out among senators when the diminutive Foote goaded the massive Benton during the latter's speech. As Benton advanced menacingly towards his antagonist, Foote stood up, drew his pistol and retreated down the aisle. Foote faced the looming Missourian as other senators rose and shouted for the intervention of the sergeant-at-arms. The presiding officer called in vain for order while pleading with members to sit down. Benton was forcibly dragged back to his seat shouting, "Stand out of the way! Let the assassin fire! I disdain to carry arms! Let him fire!" Others meanwhile had wrested the pistol out of Foote's hand and reasoned with him to return to his desk. Both men went unpunished by their colleagues. Foote, however, had learned just how far he could taunt his adversary. He never again provoked the physically daunting Benton.

When Speaker Tom Reed set a new rule of counting the quorum in the 51st Congress one member objected so strongly that he kicked open a door to get out of the House chamber. Many Democrats had already left the chamber and Rep. Constantine Buckley Kilgore (D-Tex.) was on his way out when the Speaker ordered all the doors locked until a quorum could be obtained. Miffed by the new rule, Kilgore ignored the protests of a messenger and kicked at a locked door. As it swung open it struck Rep. Nelson Dingley, Jr. (R-Me.) on the nose. The Texan apologized then stormed away from the chamber muttering, "It will take more than any door to keep me a prisoner in the House."

"Buck" Kilgore

Though Benjamin Tillman wore a glass eye in his left socket, the result of a childhood illness, his right eye locked on many a VIP he singled out for abuse. A wealthy plantation owner and former governor of South Carolina, Tillman was dubbed *Pitchfork Ben* during his successful 1894 run for the U.S. Senate when he boasted, "If I go to the Senate I promise that I will use a pitchfork in the President's fat old ribs." A violent and temperamental man, Tillman was re-elected three times even though censured for clinching and almost coming to blows with his fellow South Carolinian in the Senate chamber. Outraged, President Theodore Roosevelt withdrew his invitation for *Pitchfork Ben* to meet Prince Henry of Prussia at the White House.

Lamb's Biographical Dictionary of the U.S.

*Jefferson Davis*

*One of the thousands of Union soldiers billeted in the Capitol during the Civil War vented his rage against the South by bayonetting the mahogany Senate desk occupied by Jefferson Davis of Mississippi before he became president of the Confederacy. The soldier, a private in the 6th Massachusetts Regiment then temporarily quartered in the Senate chamber, stabbed at the desk just as assistant doorkeeper Isaac Bassett entered the historic room. "Stop that! Stop that! What are you doing?" Bassett screamed. "That is not Jeff Davis' desk. It belongs to the Government of the United States. You were sent here to protect Government property, not to destroy it!" Though the soldier withdrew, he had already scarred the desk's dark wood. Experts set about repairing it and the only remaining evidence of vandalism is a small block of wood inlay on the left-hand side.*

Rep. Preston Brooks (D-S.C.) fumed as he listened to the yankee senator make a blistering attack on his aged uncle, Sen. Andrew Butler (D-S.C.). The angry words came during a senate debate in 1856 on whether Kansas should be admitted to the Union as a free or slave state. Brooks glared at Sen. Charles Sumner (R-Mass.) as the northerner compared slavery to a harlot, whom Butler had taken as a mistress. Brooks determined to avenge the insults to his kinsman and to South Carolina. Three days later he entered the Senate chamber as it adjourned. Sumner was seated, attending to correspondence. The southerner raised his gold-topped cane and whacked Sumner on the head. The bleeding northerner tried to fend off the attack but Brooks rained down so many blows that his cane snapped. Desperate to escape, Sumner tore his desk free of its floor fastenings before collapsing unconscious. Sumner was hurt so badly that three years passed before he returned to the Senate. A move to censure Brooks failed in the House.

*Rep. Brooks assaults Sen. Sumner in the Senate, 1856*

*When Andrew Jackson was elected to the Senate in 1823 he found himself sitting several feet away from a man he had faced in a gunfight a decade earlier. Worse still, Jackson's left shoulder still bore the bullet fired from behind by a third gunman and original cause of the shootout, Sen. Thomas Benton's cowardly brother, Jesse. Ever since that violent episode in a Nashville, Tennessee hotel, Jackson and Thomas Benton, once firm friends and comrades-in-arms, had shunned each other.*

*In the Senate they continued their frigid stand-off, ignoring each other's presence until they found themselves together on a committee chaired by Jackson. They spoke briefly to one another and a few days later shook hands at a White House function. Benton later confided to a third party, "Yes, I had a fight with Jackson. A fellow was hardly in the fashion then who hadn't. But mine was different from his other fights. It wasn't about Rachel," (Jackson's wife). In a show of enduring friendship, Benton led the successful 1837 fight in the Senate to expunge from the record all reference to the censure of then President Jackson, passed three years earlier by political foes.*

*Andrew Jackson*

*Thomas Benton*

———— ▯ ————

Rep. James Roosevelt (D-Calif.), the son of Franklin and Eleanor, kept a polite and cool distance from Rep. Mendel Rivers (D-S.C.) because the two were poles apart on civil rights. Rivers had a particular antipathy towards the congressman's mother because of her strong advocacy of civil rights. One day Rivers addressed the House and made an abusive remark about Eleanor Roosevelt, knowing that her son was seated only a few rows behind. Enraged, Roosevelt was about to leap over the seats and scuffle with Rivers when other congressmen talked him out of it. Rivers, however, realized how far out of line he had gone. When he reviewed the draft edition of that day's Congressional Record he wisely omitted the inflammatory remarks.

*G*unshots fired across the street from the White House snuffed out a high society love triangle that scandalized Washington and derailed the presidential hopes of a celebrity congressman. For almost a year many insiders knew what Rep. Daniel Sickles, 40, was blind to: his coy wife, Teresa, 23, was having a torrid affair with the U.S. attorney for the District of Columbia, Philip Barton Key, whom one senator's wife described as "the handsomest man in all Washington society."

The tall and dapper Key had a pedigree linking him to distinguished citizens, including an uncle, Chief Justice Taney and a socially prominent brother-in-law, Rep. George Pendleton. Above all, he was the son of the legendary Francis Scott Key, whose poetry became the words of the Star-Spangled Banner.

Key met Teresa and Daniel Sickles (D-N.Y.) at a festive inaugural ball in 1858 for incoming President James Buchanan. The fateful introduction quickly led to an amorous liaison even as the unwitting congressman used his influence with the new president, whose secretary he had been when Buchanan was Minister in the U.S. legation in London, to reconfirm Key as the U.S. attorney for the District of Columbia.

*Teresa Sickles*

*The lovers met in this rented house*

*Key became a frequent guest at the Sickles' white brick home on fashionable Lafayette Square, directly opposite the White House. And he often partnered the black-haired Teresa, daughter of an Italian immigrant musician, at weekly dances in nearby Willard's Hotel. But less than three weeks after they first met rumor reached the gruff congressman that his wife and Key had been seen horse-riding together and checking into an inn. They escaped exposure only because the original witness lost his nerve when confronted by the wayward district attorney. Daniel Sickles, himself a notorious philanderer, accepted Key's innocence after reading the frightened witness's written retraction.*

Key was still welcome in the congressman's three-story home but he and Teresa continued to flaunt their relationship with reckless indiscretion. Throughout the spring and early summer society gossips watched them dancing together. Her staff knew of his late night visits to the Sickles home when the congressman was out of town. Her knowing coachman whisked her to the Congressional Cemetery where Key lay in wait. And in the fall they frolicked at a secret rendezvous just blocks away from her home. Key had rented an empty house, telling the owner and neighbors that he was merely an agent for a senator. Their curiosity aroused, neighbors peeked out of windows and saw the furtive comings and goings of the lovers.

Key and Teresa, the mother of a three-year-old daughter, were even less circumspect in communicating with one another. He was frequently in Lafayette Square, ostensibly to visit the posh National Club diagonally opposite the Sickles home. He made no effort to conceal himself from observers as he stood outside signaling with a wave of his white handkerchief while Teresa watched from her home. The district attorney picked up her answering codes by focusing his opera glasses on her upstairs window. Driven as if by compulsion towards a showdown, Key ignored the warnings of those aware of the gossip, denying there was anything untoward in his friendship for Teresa.

The boom fell towards the end of winter 1859. Sickles had just hosted a dinner party at his home when he opened a letter signed mysteriously by "Your friend R.P.G." In halting English made worse by grammatical errors, the tattler told of Key's liasons with "your wife" in the rented house where "he hangs a string out of the window as a signal to her that he is in and leaves the door unfastened and she walks in......with these few hints I leave the rest for you to imagine."

Sickles' disbelief turned to thunderous rage when he and a snooping friend confirmed the worst by questioning the household staff and neighbors used to scanning activities at the rented rendezvous several blocks away. Two days after receiving R.P.G.'s note Sickles roared his findings to a weeping Teresa and then compelled her to sign a long and detailed confession of infidelity.

Distraught to the point of tears himself, Sickles was at home the following day pouring out his grief to trusted confidants when he looked out the window and saw Key in the street below waving his white handerchief in the direction of the upstairs window. "That villain!" he fumed.

Sickles raced for his pistols and dashed out and around the square as Key approached the National Club. Unmindful of stunned witnesses, the cuckolded

The victim's opera glasses

congressman screamed, "Key, you scoundrel! You have dishonored my bed! You must die!" He fired one shot but missed as Key scrambled for cover behind a tree. "Don't shoot!" Key pleaded as Sickles squeezed the trigger and missed again. Pathetically, Key threw his opera glasses at his assailant then fell wounded as two more bullets struck home. Sickles came closer to administer the coup de grace with a bullet to the head but his weapon jammed. Wit-

*The Congressman shoots to death his wife's lover*

nesses temporarily frozen by the drama now stepped forward and overpowered Sickles. They carried the wounded man into the National Club but within minutes he was dead.

Five weeks later Sickles went on trial for murder. From the Atlantic to the Pacific coasts Americans feasted on sensational newspaper accounts of every lurid detail of the crime passionnel. A bevy of high-powered defense lawyers successfully pleaded that their client's rage and grief over his wife's adultery had rendered him temporarily insane when he shot Key. Spectators greeted the acquittal with three cheers and more than a thousand supporters later mobbed the triumphant Sickles.

Theresa lived out her remaining years in New York, branded and snubbed, according to the mores of the time, as a disgraced woman. Though they did not divorce they seldom lived together. Just eight years after her lover was gunned down, Theresa herself lay dead of natural causes.

Sickles lived on adventurously for 47 additional years, becoming even more of a celebrity. Slaying Key put paid to any hopes he may have had about running for president but it did not sandbag the remaining years of accomplishment. He was a major general during the Civil War and won the Medal of Honor at Gettysburg for "vigorously contesting the advance of the enemy and continuing to encourage his troops after being himself severely wounded." When a cannonball shattered his right leg and surgeons amputated it above the knee, he sent the severed limb with his compliments to the Armed Forces Medical Museum in Washington, D.C. In 1869 he was named Minister to Spain and made frequent trips from Madrid to Paris where he became one of the many lovers of exiled Queen Isabella 11. In 1871 he married a Spaniard who had once served in Isabella's court, but eight years later abandoned her and their son and daughter when he returned to the United States to become chairman of the New York State Civil Service Commission. Later he was appointed head of the New York State Monuments Commission and in 1892 won reelection to a third term in Congress.

When Sickles was 70 years old he inherited several million dollars from his father's real estate and other investments. Wealth enabled him to gamble for high stakes and to indulge the opposite sex. He squandered so much that when he died in 1914 at the age of 94 he was broke.

*Sickles was jailed briefly immediately after the shooting*

# A MOTLEY LOT

---□---

*I think there are members (of Congress) that you wouldn't hire
to wheel a wheelbarrow.*

*-- Rep. Sam Steiger (R-Ariz.) 1967*

John Sparkman seldom went to bed without raiding the refrigerator
for a glass of buttermilk into which he crumbled cornbread. So far so
good. But the Alabaman, who served 42 years in Congress and was the
Democratic vice presidential nominee in 1952, always chased his night-
cap with hot peppers. It was obviously good for his system. He lived on
to celebrate his 85th birthday.

---□---

*Capitol Hill pages got rare glimpses of distinguished senators caught off
guard when out of the public eye. An eccentric who made an indelible impression
was Sen. John Hamilton Lewis of Illinois. He was already in the public eye
because of his pink toupee, whiskers and moustache and the way he flourished his
cane with joyous ostentation. What stuck most in the mind of one observant
page, Donald Detwiler, was the way Lewis prepared an envelope for mailing.
"He would lick the envelope and then put the stamp on it."*

*Talk about thick-skinned politicians. Sen. Thomas Hart Benton (D-Mo.) had his servant scrub him down with a horse-hair brush twice a day to emulate a custom of the Roman gladiators. Every morning the proud and physically powerful senator had the top half of his body bathed and scrubbed with the coarse brush. In the afternoons Benton, a former lieutenant colonel, braced himself for a scrubbing from his hips to his feet. The daily ritual was apparently good for his health. When he died in 1858 he was a ripe old 76.*

Sen. William Proxmire was one of the most long-winded men ever to sit in Congress. It had nothing to do with long speeches. The Wisconsin Democrat was a fitness freak. Apparently he wasn't satisfied with running a mere five miles daily from his Washington home to his office in the U.S. Capitol. When he got back to his home state he passed the winter of 1975 running around Wisconsin's entire frozen 700-mile perimeter.

Senators found a fitting nickname for one of their finicky, fussy mid-20th century colleagues. Francis Case (R-S.D.) used to peer intently at the language and punctuation of every bill as it passed through the many stages before the final vote. At the last moment, it would not trouble Case to hold up a measure by suggesting the inclusion of a semi-colon to perfect its intent. With good humor, other senators soon came to refer to him as "Semi-colon Case."

*Reporters race from press gallery to file their stories.*

Nothing seemed to get under Sen. Burton Wheeler's skin more than free-wheeling newspaper writers who covered Congress. When two of the newsmen put out a story in 1940 reflecting badly on Democratic party finances, Wheeler (D-Mont.) took the offensive. He demanded that journalists who publicly ridiculed members of Congress should be barred from the press galleries. "People must have respect for members of the Senate and the House," he declared, "especially in these times when there is a trend to totalitarianism throughout the country." Wheeler never got anywhere with his suggestion but it enabled him to let off accumulated steam.

**V**ermont Republican Winston Prouty had an abiding chill whenever he had to campaign because of a severed right thumb. The childhood accident at the family's lumber and building material plant left him with a lifelong psychological scar. If photographed in a group he kept his right hand behind his back. Prouty's self-consciousness told every time he had to shake hands with strangers. Yet he still managed to win four elections to the House and three more to the Senate before his death in 1971.

Senators George Pepper (R-Pa.), George Moses (R-N.H.), George Norris (R-Neb.), George McLean (R-Conn.), and Walter George (D-Ga.) had one thing in common. They didn't like the name George being loosely bandied about. Every Tom, Dick and Harry, it seemed, called all sleeping car and parlor car porters 'George'. So in 1924 they immediately signed on as members of a newly-formed Society for the Prevention of Calling Pullman Car Porters 'George'. Appropriately, the society's patron was George Washington.

No woman left more of a mark on the House of Representatives than feisty Bella Abzug (D-N.Y.), "the voice of the voiceless" and champion of women's rights, who served a mere six years. Hardly ever without her wide-brimmed floppy hats, she was flamboyant, colorful and admired for her legislative skills. Twenty six colleagues rose to lament her departure in 1976. Her greatest legacy, according to humorist Mo Udall (D-Ariz.) was how "she changed us from congressmen to congresspersons, from gentlemen to gentlepersons, from a men's club to a place where a woman could walk without fear of having a mop flung at her." Rep. Louis Stokes (D-Ohio), a former chairman of the Congressional Black Caucus, recalled Abzug's memorable brush with perky House doorman William Mosley 'Fishbait' Miller. "When once requested by "Fishbait" to remove her hat, Bella cutely suggested that Mr. Miller perform an impossible act. This was classic Bella."

*When the Republicans took control of the Senate in 1947 octogenrian Sen. Kenneth McKellar (D-Tenn.) had a hard time remembering he had lost his position as president pro tem. Capitol Hill police watched boggle-eyed as the aged senator walked into the empty chamber on Saturdays, mounted the rostrum and sat down in the presiding officer's chair. The police gently nudged him out of the chamber by telling him, "Senator, they just called to say they're not going to be in today." Puzzled, McKellar responded, "Oh, they're not?" At other times the police found the elderly senator in the wrong wing of the Capitol, trying to take the elevator up to the House of Representatives. On such occasions the lawmen guided him slowly over to the Senate wing.*

*T*he heaviest man ever elected to Congress weighed more than 400 lbs. Sen. Dixon Hall Lewis (D-Ala.) shied away from making speeches in the summer because, as he confided, "I am so big and fat that you would have to fan me and that would not be very dignified." He suffered no such shame when first elected and made pages fan him in hourly shifts. Horse-drawn carriage drivers made excuses not to carry him after he once fell through the floorboards onto the street. Some boarding-house keepers charged him double rates to make up for the quantity of food he consumed, while other landlords refused to rent him rooms. Born in 1802, the bulky lawyer had a chair twice as large as the others. He died aged 46, apparently due to overweight.

*Dixon Hall Lewis*

Contemporaries of Sen. Charles Thomas of Colorado had no need of spring crocuses or falling autumn leaves to signal the change of seasons. All they had to do was look at Thomas' head. If it was spring, the Colorado Democrat would have a shiny bald pate. And so it would remain, all through the clammy Washington summers. But with the coming of the autumn chill, senators would suddenly notice the changed appearance of their colleague. It was the time of year when he stuck on his toupee to keep him warm until the end of winter.

---

*Zachariah Chandler*

*Sen. Zachariah Chandler (R-Mich.) never let long, dull night sessions get the better of him. He simply lay down on one of the sofas in the Senate chamber and fell into a deep sleep. Generally the debates continued without distraction because his snores were tolerably low. On one occasion, though, he snored so loudly that the vice president asked veteran assistant doorman, Isaac Bassett, to wake Chandler. Bassett shook the large man several times but the snoring continued. Dutifully, Bassett took hold of one of the senator's legs and pulled on it violently.*

*"What do you want?" Chandler asked grumpily. "Are they voting?"*

*"No, sir," Bassett replied respectfully, "but you snored so loud that you disturbed the Senate."*

*"Well I'm going to snore till they adjourn," Chandler rebuked. With that he lay down and resumed his sleep.*

Sen. Theodore Green (D-R.I) used to recount why he never put off for tomorrow what had to be done today. It had saved his life when he was a young man. He was in the parlor car of a train leaving Chicago, writing letters to people he had left behind. After sealing the letters in envelopes he realized he could not give them to the conductor to mail at the next stop, as he usually did, because he had left his postage stamps back in his berth. At first he thought of pocketing the letters and mailing them the following day. Then he decided to get the stamps immediately. The change of mind saved his life. He was back in his berth when the train was involved in a collision. Everyone inside the parlor car was killed.

*P*erle Mesta's popularity as Washington's pre-eminent hostess paid off when her nomination as ambassador to Luxembourg came up for Senate confirmation in 1949. For years she had entertained the nation's power elite at lavish parties. Not surprisingly, only one senator protested her lack of qualifications. But Sen. Forrest Donnell (R-Mo.) went too far when he called the Foreign Relations Committee to task for not summoning Mrs. Mesta to appear before it. This stung Sen. Charles Tobey (R- N.H.). "She has not come before the committee, but the senators have come before Perle Mesta many a time," he chided. The lady's finest moment came when Foreign Relations Committee chairman Tom Connally compared her with Foreign Service career men who, he said, got into ruts, broke routinely for 4 o'clock tea, and wore the same kind of clothes. "I rather favor bringing some fresh air from the outside," he added. On a voice vote, every senator agreed, with the exception of Donnell.

There was nothing wishy-washy about Allen Ellender's likes and dislikes. Upon his election to the Senate in 1936, the Louisiana Democrat was told to submit three choices for committee assignments. He wrote "Agriculture, Agriculture, Agriculture." Such was his zeal that he created history serving on the committee. For 18 years he served as chairman - longer than any of his 40 predecessors since the first was named in 1825.

Sen. Lister Hill (D-Ala.) always cleared big decisions with his red-headed twin sister. After John F. Kennedy's assassination he had to eulogize the slain president and ordered senior aide Stuart McClure to write the speech over the weekend. McClure and a friend got to work, aware of JFK's unpopularity in Alabama. They built the speech around the senators' shared pursuit of excellence, and described Kennedy as a man of peace, a theme that could not hurt Hill back in Alabama since Kennedy had signed a test-ban treaty with the Soviets. Hill looked it over then sent it down to his twin for clearance. A few days later he exulted, "My red-headed twin sister says it's the best speech she's read since Cicero! We'll go ahead with it!"

Sen. David Davis momentarily forgot that he weighed almost 400 lbs. as he stepped down from the presiding officer's rostrum to stretch his legs. He shuffled slowly around the chamber before settling into a chair belonging to a lightweight senator. The wooden seat came apart and the former supreme court justice tumbled to the floor for the third time since his election to the Senate in 1877. A colleague seated nearby smiled as Davis, mortified, overheard another senator label him "the jumbo of the Senate." After he raised himself, Davis (Indep-Ill.) circled the chamber several times to regain his composure. But he was unforgiving of those who made fun of his misfortune. He refused to accept the apologies offered by the man caught smiling. After a previous spill, he shunned a senator for an entire week because the man had dared chuckle.

---

**Rep. Joseph Bryson (D-S.C.) boasted a larger private collection of Bibles than any of his peers in the history of Congress. When he counted them in 1950 he had 100 in as many languages. In all, his library comprised 30,000 volumes. Bryson's oldest Bible was printed in England in 1608.**

---

*Sam Houston's first marriage was the saddest romance in the annals of Congress. He was already 36 and his bride, Eliza Allen, only 18 when they married in 1829. It ended two months later. Houston abruptly resigned the governorship of Tennessee and rode off alone to lick his wounds with a tribe of friendly Cherokee Indians. He never gave a reason for the sudden rupture and divorce four years later. By most accounts Houston found out that his young wife had married him only to please her father, and that she was still in love with another man. Stunned, he decided to end the marriage, telling her he could not be married to a slave. Houston, forever a ladies man, was romantically linked with several women before remarrying in 1840, six years before his election to the Senate.*

The 51st Congress passed so many laws that as soon as the Speaker gaveled it to a close in 1891 members celebrated vacation time by bursting into song. Republicans grouped around the front row desks to give a rousing rendition of the Civil War classic, *Marching Through Georgia*. Not to be outdone, Democratic lungs bellowed the words of *Home, Sweet Home*. Before they had even finished they were drowned out by songsters in the press gallery singing *Praise God From Whom All Blessings Flow*. Astonished spectators in the galleries joined in the fun, singing along with those below. More than an hour passed before the last of the warbling legisla tors left for home and a long break from Washington.

———————————□———————————

It was not uncommon for 19th century senators to be floored without violence. During a dull speech in sweltering August, Sen. George Hoar (R-Mass.) swayed back and forth in a tilted cane chair as he read the newspaper after lunch. Suddenly he lost his balance and flipped backwards onto the floor. An onlooker tittered in the public gallery and proceedings stopped. The assistant doorkeeper, who had been called upon many times in the past to help senators to their feet, rushed in to repeat his skills. Other senators sniggered as the weighty Hoar settled himself in his chair and got on with his reading.

*I*t was during the roaring twenties, with big bucks to be made bootlegging whisky in defiance of Prohibition laws. Eight-term Rep. John Wesley Langley (R-Ky.) didn't want to be left out. He was earning only $7,500 as a U.S. Representative. Yet, said the district attorney at Langley's trial on charges of conspiring to sell whisky illegally, the congressman had banked $115,000 in his accounts over a three year period. The prosecution told of the illegal removal of 1,400 cases of whiskey from a Kentucky distillery. Records had been fixed showing the whiskey was to be sold for medicinal purposes while the real intent was to sell it as beverage. The Governor of Kentucky and two congressmen spoke highly in court of Langley's reputation, though all three said he drank too much. Langley was convicted and sentenced to two years in the penitentiary. It didn't sit well with his constituents - staunch Republican mountain folk who thought their man was being persecuted. They reelected him while he appealed the verdict. When the supreme court gave Langley the thumbs down in 1926, he resigned from Congress and went to jail. The voters promptly elected his wife, Katherine. Eleven months later President Coolidge pardoned Langley.

———□———

A strange taste in the Bourbon had Kentucky's two U.S. Senators placing bets on what it could be. Interest in the outcome was keen because both James Beck and Joseph Blackburn claimed to be connoisseurs of whiskey. Beck insisted there must have been a piece of leather in the barrel of bourbon given to him by a stranger. No, said Blackburn. It tasted of iron. It took them two months to finish the barrel and look for the cause. But neither man claimed victory. When they looked inside they found an iron carpet tack with a leather head.

The only female awarded a Medal of Honor battled Congress for years over the right of women to dress in men's more comfortable clothing. Many contemporaries dismissed Dr. Mary Walker, a former Civil War army surgeon, as an eccentric crackpot. She was once arrested in New York City for wearing men's pants under a skirt. When she demanded Congress pay for her government medical services, she was turned down, according to word reaching her, because of her unorthodox dress. The fei-

*Dr. Mary Walker*

sty crusader responded sarcastically, demanding a constitutional amendment for the recruitment of a national costumer from a foreign court to outfit American women appropriately. Appearing before the House Judiciary Committee in 1912, she scotched a widely reported story that Congress had given her the right to wear men's clothes."I want this (rumor) forever stopped," she snapped.

Leonard Hall was never awed by high office, even though he himself had a distinguished career as a congressman from New York before becoming chairman of the Republican National Committee. So when he later became a judge he rebuked a court attendant who helped him on with his robes and obsequiously called him "Your Honor", even though they had been at high school together. One day Hall summoned the man and said with a smile, "Call me Your Honor when you're in the courtroom. But, you SOB, if you ever call me Your Honor in my chambers, you're going to be fired that day!"

* * *

Card games have lured Capitol Hill legislators and staff like moths to lighted bulbs but none went to such marathon lengths as the celebrated game held in 1832. Capitol Hill buzzed with accounts of the game that began after Congress adjourned on a Thursday and continued on, with only a brief respite for 40 winks, until the legislature resumed business on Monday morning. One of the players, Governor Stokes of North Carolina, was all for playing on well into the new week. However, Mountjoy Bailey, the Senate's sergeant-at-arms, protested that his official duties required his presence on the Hill. Stokes continued to remonstrate as Bailey got up and left. When the fatigued Bailey appeared in the Senate chamber a colleague reported that "he attended to his duties as usual."

*If disaster struck and Senate president pro tempore, Warren Magnuson found himself succeeding to the presidency, he made it clear he would not go anywhere in the first fateful hours unless his wife joined him. Magnuson (D-Wash.) was third in line to the presidency, after the vice president and speaker of the House of Representatives, when elected to preside over the Senate in 1979. Immediately the Secret Service primed him on procedures to be followed if he became president and had to be evacuated out of Washington. During such an emergency he would have to board a helicopter. If his wife was present she could also take the flight. "Well if she isn't with me, I'm not getting aboard," Magnuson vowed. He said they would have to take a car, pick up his wife and drive both of them to wherever they had to go.*

North Carolina Sen. Clyde Hoey cut a strikingly patrician figure in his winged collars and swallowtail coat but nothing caught so much attention as the fresh red rose in his lapel. Never a day passed without the tall senator sporting his favorite flower. When he died in the spring of 1954 he was eulogized in the Senate chamber. None of the tributes proved more moving than the gesture of an anonymous admirer who placed a single red rose on the senator's empty desk.

───────□───────

**Sen. Sam Houston of Texas never had breakfast until he had downed four cocktails, according to a contemporary newspaper account. The same correspondent described Sen. Thomas Benton's favorite drink as the Missouri cocktail - "a double portion of whiskey straight."**

*House Speaker Charles Crisp (D-Ga.) never spoke to anyone until he had finished his breakfast, his theory being that no one could be himself until all parts of his body were in working order. The popular, plain-living Crisp got out of bed punctually at 7 a.m., read the newspapers and then breakfasted alone at 8 a.m. Yet he was anything but a boring loner. The Speaker was noted for his rolicking enjoyment of good jokes. He liked nothing better than to roar with laughter at the many jokes told him by congressmen dropping by his office. A down-to-earth man, Crisp shunned late 19th century private carriages and horses, preferring to ride public transport at all times. And he turned down almost every social invitation in favor of spending the time with his wife at their unpretentious hotel rooms.*

Major General Sam Houston's flamboyant outfits assured him a lasting place among the most colorfully attired senators. Elected to the Senate after the lone star state's admission to the Union he was immediately conspicuous for his clothing. Houston was seldom without his grey felt Mexican sombrero with its eight inch wide brim. More riveting were the panther and tiger-skin vests and voluminous scarlet neck-ties. In the cooler seasons he draped a multi-colored, scarlet-lined Mexican serape over his broad shoulders.

Years earlier he had frequently dressed in the full costume of an Indian warrior, wearing a headdress of turkey feathers, a brilliantly-embroidered white hunting shirt, yellow leggings and beaded moccassins. At a treaty-making council with Indians he wore a suit of purple velvet embossed with animal-head representations. Tucked in his belt was a large bowie knife. Houston's simple explanation for the striking costume was that it would awe the Indians and impress them with the belief that he was a great warrior.

# ONE-UPMANSHIP

---□---

*We've got more egos up there on the Hill than we've got any place else in the world. And if you can handle those, you can handle anybody.*

*-- Nordy Hoffman, Senate sergeant-at-arms, 1975-1981*

President Franklin Roosevelt once teased House minority leader Joe Martin that he had set a trap for Republicans in a forthcoming state of the Union message, "so make sure you don't cheer in the wrong places." After the address the president asked, "Well, Joe, did you cheer in the wrong places?" It was Martin's turn to laugh. "No, Mr. President, we didn't cheer at all."

---□---

*Wright Patman (D-Tex.) served for so long in the House of Representatives that when he died in his 48th year in congress, a mourner told a humorous story by way of tribute. It concerned a young lawyer who had been foolish enough to run against Patman years before and been soundly defeated. Undaunted, the same lawyer then took on the district attorney, deriding his opponent as a man who had not even completed high school. Trumpeted the young lawyer, "I am a graduate of the Harvard Law School!" The elderly district attorney quickly admitted he had little education and that perhaps he had no business running for elective office. Then came the punch line. "I do not have much sense but I have always had sense enough never to run against Wright Patman."*

Louisiana Democrat Huey "Kingfish" Long loved to rib some of his Senate colleagues, particularly Kenneth McKellar of Tennessee, because he got so mad so quickly. One day Long had the public galleries in stitches as he needled the obviously irate McKellar. The presiding officer threatened to oust the public unless they quietened down. At that point Kentucky's Sen. Alben Barkley got a dig in at Long by saying, "When the people go to a circus they ought to be allowed to laugh at the monkey." Long was quick to turn the tables. Rising, he said, "I resent that unwarranted remark on the part of the senator from Kentucky, directed toward my good friend, the senator from Tennesee!"

---

**The debate on national defense and security had droned on tiresomely until Rep. John Riley (D-S.C.) took the floor and told of an incident in the life of one of his friends. "He was visiting in one of our large cities and as he walked down a more or less deserted street a gunman stuck a rod in his ribs and demanded, 'Your money or your life!' 'Take my life!' said my excited friend. 'I am saving my money for my old age.'"**

*E*ven though Senate majority leader, Lyndon Johnson got along well with his friend, minority leader Everett Dirksen, they thrived on a spirit of one-upmanship. One evening Dirksen spotted Johnson leaving Capitol Hill in his chauffeur-driven car. What caught his eye was Johnson using the new-fangled car telephone. Impressed, Dirksen ordered one for his car without delay. At a convenient moment, Dirksen had his chauffeur drive parallel to Johnson's car then he dialed the majority leader. "Lyndon, isn't this a great idea to have these phones in the car so we can talk this way," said Dirksen. "Yes," replied Johnson, "but excuse me Ev, I've got to answer the other phone."

Emanuel Celler's 48 years in Congress taught him how to make short shrift of bigots and fools. One man who fit the description and suffered the consequences was John Rankin (D-Miss.). After Rankin made one of many speeches shafting Jews, Celler, a New York Democrat and proud Jew, described the remarks as a canard. Rankin protested to Speaker Sam Rayburn who consulted the dictionary, found that canard meant a lie and ordered the remark stricken as unparliamentary. A few days later when Rankin made another anti-Semitic slur, Celler denounced it, comparing it to "the criminal who returns to the scene of his crime or the sow that returns to her wallow." Stung, Rankin asked for Celler's remarks to be stricken. The Speaker asked Celler, "Has the gentleman from New York any reason to disclose why the words are not unparliamentary?" Replied Celler: "The words are from the Bible." "Well," said Speaker Rayburn to a gleeful Celler, "if they're from the Bible they're not unparliamentary."

**H**erbert Hoover's dour countenance masked a devilish sense of humor. One day the Republican president sent a picture of himself to House Democratic leader John Garner. Above the presidential autograph was the inscription: To John Garner, with good wishes in every possible direction except politics.

*They were both Harvard men but one delivered such a matchless put-down of the other that it has survived since delivered at the turn of the 19th century. Sen. Edward Wolcott (R-Colo.) one of the finest orators of his time, was explaining why the speeches of Sen. Henry Cabot Lodge (R-Mass.) left men cold. "To bring tears from an audience," said Wolcott, "the speaker must feel tears here (pointing to his throat). But Lodge can speak for an hour with nothing but saliva in his throat."*

John Hale

*A*nti-slavery advocate, Sen. John Hale, was so good natured that he turned the tables even on those who wanted him dead. The New Hampshire legislator gave proof of this before the Civil War when goaded by Sen. Henry Foote of Mississippi. Foote warned Hale he would be hanged from the tallest tree if he came to Mississippi. Unruffled, Hale promised an hospitable welcome for Foote in New Hampshire. Foote would be shown all the churches and free schools and free laborers. If Foote still remained unimpressed, the people of New Hampshire would not hang him. Instead, said Hale with tongue-in-cheek, they would hire a hall for the Mississippian and let him talk as long as he pleased, certain that if given enough rope he would hang himself.

Plain-speaking, down-to-earth Andrew Jackson put a senator in his place with delicious finesse. The story is told of an English noblewoman visiting Washington who asked Sen. James Buchanan (D-Pa.) to arrange an audience with President Jackson. Buchanan, who himself became president 20 years after Jackson, was warmly received by the chief executive but made the mistake of emphasizing that the Englishwoman was accustomed to the social niceties of her rank. "Buchanan," rebuked the famed soldier from Tennessee, "when I went to school I read about a man that I was much interested in. He was a man who minded his own business." Imagine Buchanan's surprise when later that day the president came down the steps of the White House in formal dress to welcome the English aristocrat. More astonishing to the senator was the lady's comment upon leaving the White House. "Why did you not prepare me for this?" she asked Buchanan. "In all my travels I have not met a more elegant gentleman."

———————— ⊡ ————————

*The three Republicans in the Wisconsin primary were given a few minutes each to sell themselves as the best qualified candidate for Congress. The first two were lawyers. One boasted he knew Washington well because he'd been there on party work. The second claimed he'd navigated a ship around the world and therefore would have no difficulty finding his way around the nation's capital. The third candidate was a congregational minister, Rev. Henry Schadeberg. "If I go to Congress I promise that if a legal matter comes up I will obtain the best legal advice possible," he said, "but I doubt whether any lawyer will ever ask for any moral advice." After the laughter died down Schadeberg won the primary and the 1960 election.*

A number of liberal Massachusetts clergy didn't bargain for an explosive surprise when they marched on the office of their congressman, Rep. Hastings Keith, a supporter of the administration's Vietnam war policies. But Keith (R) had done his homework. He knew that the delegation's leader had recently announced his intention of divorcing his wife to marry another parishioner. Keith let his visitors take the offensive then compared the U.S. commitment to South Vietnam with solemn marriage vows. The alliance could not be scrapped just because things were going badly. "How do you feel about it?" he asked mischievously. Caught off guard, the delegation's leader mumbled something about there being merit to Keith's position.

*When Soviet leader Nikita Krushchev addressed the United Nations and pounded his shoe on the lectern, Adlai Stevenson asked his friend, Rep. Brooks Hays (D-Ark.) what he thought of the spectacle. "I think he over-egged his puddin," said Hays. "Where'd you get that expression?" asked the erudite Stevenson. Hays said it was an old Tennessee expression. That same night British foreign secretary Harold Macmillan said on a radio interview in New York that, "in the language of an old British saying, Mr. Krushchev over-egged his pudding." Hays dashed off a note to Stevenson: "Whether or not Macmillan was speaking out of his own English lore or you gave it to him, it proves that the roots of Appalachian life are deep in Elizabethan culture."*

Sen. Sam Ervin, Jr. was traveling down to North Carolina with a friend listening to the car radio when a commentator began describing the main features of a Revenue Bill under discussion in the Senate. "I don't know who's talking, but I recognize by his accent that he's a Southerner," said Ervin. "That's you, senator!" the friend remarked. "If that's right," Ervin parried, "I can say for the first time since I went to the Senate, I agree with everything that's being said."

*Sen. Stephen Young of Ohio gave as good as he got. He was particularly adept at turning the tables on constituents who sent him barbed letters. When the President of Pakistan presented a thoroughbred horse to First Lady Jacqueline Kennedy and the U.S. Air Force transported it free, an irate Ohioan protested to Young, "I require that you procure a horse for me and have it brought to me in the same manner." Young acknowledged receiving the letter insulting the wife of the U.S. President and added, "I am wondering why you need a horse when there is already one jackass at your address."*

———————— ▯ ————————

Though chairman of the formidable Atomic Investigating Committee, Sen. Bourke Hickenlooper (R-Iowa) was far from humorless. He enjoyed telling the story of a visiting Briton. "The old fellow who was guiding him around Boston took him to Bunker Hill, where the famous battle occurred. When the Briton got there he adjusted his glasses and looked over the battlefield and said to the guide, 'Is not this the place where we British gave you Yankees such a drubbing in '76?' The old fellow who was guiding him said, 'I am not too familiar with the details of history, but who owns the ground now!'"

**S**enate Democratic Leader Lyndon Johnson loved to josh verbally with his Republican counterpart, Everett Dirksen of Illinois. One day the future president from Texas made light of Dirksen's wishy-washy stand by telling a joke about a teacher who applied for a job in the backwoods. The school board chairman told him the community was split on geography and wanted to know where the job-hunter stood. Did he teach that the world was flat or that the world was round? With an aw shucks attitude, the teacher replied, "I can teach it either way."

Freshman Rep. Charles Gubser (R-Calif.) got trumped by a British communist after visiting divided Berlin. Deeply impressed after seeing the exodus of more than a thousand refugees a day from East Germany, Gubser stopped over in London. There he unwisely took on one of the skilled outdoor soap-box orators at Hyde Park's famous Speakers' Corner. "If communism is as good as you say it is why are they leaving?" asked Gubser. Replied the communist, "You are just like any other American. You put yourself where you saw what you wanted to see. Had you tried you would have seen two thousand going back!"

Sen. William Proxmire (D-Wis.) was a pastmaster at the gentle art of one-upmanship. In 1971 a columnist for the Cincinnati Enquirer fired a broadside at him for wanting to get the government out of the supersonic transport business. As a penalty for such nonsense, the columnist suggested a nationwide boycott of Wisconsin dairy products because "Wisconsin cows are dirty animals." Proxmire decided not to defend his home state's dairy industry claiming it would make as much sense as defending Beethoven as a composer or Babe Ruth as a ballplayer. "My best recourse," he told the Senate, "is to permit the good citizens of the Queen City to enjoy the humor of their morning newspaper jester without interference. To err, after all, really is human."

*New York's maverick congressman, Vito Marcantonio, often raised the hackles of his colleagues with his pro-Soviet politics but he could be just as scathing with his critics. His tongue darted when Rep. John Taber (R-N.Y.) took the Library of Congress to task in 1948 for publishing a monthly list of new Russian books "that will be very convenient for the Commies to examine." Marcantonio, an American Laborite, suggested that Taber, a Yale graduate and chairman of the Committee on Appropriations, "recommend a reasonable amount of money to provide for the burning of the books."*

As far as Katherine St. George was concerned, politics was thicker than blood. Even though first cousin Franklin Delano Roosevelt was running for president, she could not vote for him because he was a Democrat and she was a Republican. Piqued, her uncle Fred Delano wrote her hoping that "in spite of your political affiliation, you will vote for your cousin." St. George, who was later elected to Congress as a New York Republican, replied, "Dear Uncle Fred, I'm greatly honored that my cousin Franklin should be nominated for president of the United States. I would be equally honored if you were nominated pope of Rome, but I would not for that reason become a Roman Catholic."

*Democrat John Gaines of Tennessee got boyish kicks out of throwing Republicans off balance by interrupting their speeches with complex questions. But humorist Charles Landis (R-Ind.) came well prepared to turn the tables in the 58th Congress. As Gaines stood up to throw in the red herring, Landis held up a piece of paper for all to see. To much laughter, Landis asked Gaines whether "he is the author of this bill, introduced to repeal the war taxes six months after the war taxes were wiped off of the statute books?" Mortified, Gaines sat down without a peep.*

Jim Fulton's puckish sense of humor saw him through one of the most strained periods of his long political life. Even though his Pennsylvania district was heavily labor, he voted in favor of the Taft-Hartley Act of 1947 which severely restricted the power of unions. Republican Fulton made light of his vote by joking that when he got back to his district a prominent union official was waiting for him. "Jim, I have a bone to pick with you." Expecting the worst, Fulton asked, "Are you going to forgive me for voting for the Taft-Hartley Act?" The union man looked hard at Fulton. "Well, Jim, we boys got together and we agreed that we are going to go along with you because everybody has got a right to make one mistake; but son, that was yours."

When Rep. Stuyvesant Wainwright 11 (R-N.Y.) called for an official home for the vice president of the United States, multi-millionaire Joseph Davies offered Tregaron, his 27-acre estate with mansion. Davies, ex-ambassador to the Soviet Union and former husband of heiress Marjorie Merriweather Post, didn't even want any money for it. Wainwright talked it over with President Eisenhower and asked him if he would look over the mansion. Ike declined. He told Wainwright that Tregaron was a much finer home than the White House and that there was no way the vice president could live in a better place than the president.

*Rep. Clare Boothe Luce (R-Conn.) put a fellow New Englander on the spot when she asked Rep. Charles Gifford (R-Mass.) if he had any formula to prevent a fool from losing his money. Gifford rose to the occasion, unintimidated by the sharp intellect and delicate beauty of the congresswoman. "A fool and his money are invited places. I do not know how anybody could prevent him from accepting invitations. I know I would not refuse if the gentlewoman invited me to go places. I could perhaps not be regarded as a fool, however, in that instance. No wise man could resist. The fool, when he travels and has money, is called a tourist."*

A couple of words of praise from Republican Sen. Wallace White of Maine for Democratic Sen. Alben Barkley of Kentucky resulted in a little bit of partisan banter between the two. "I thank the senator from Maine," said Barkley. "This episode gives me hope and encouragement to believe that hereafter the senator from Maine may have many occasions to endorse something done by a Democratic administration." To which White replied, "I do not expect to be overworked, but I shall try to meet my obligations in that respect."

Wooing a senator's daughter could be perilous but not for John "The Pathfinder" Fremont, who turned banishment to his advantage. When influential Sen. Thomas Hart Benton of Missouri saw that Fremont had his eyes on fair daughter Jessie, he "arranged" for the young Army engineer to be posted out of the nation's capital to make a survey of the far-off Des Moines River. To Fremont, the order was anything but a downer. It merely fed his lust for adventure and exploration. When he was done he returned to Washington, D.C. and in 1841 eloped with Jessie. In time, Benton came to accept his son-in-law, who became more famous in his own right, especially for his explorations west of the Rocky Mountains. In 1850 Fremont won election to the U.S. Senate from California and years later became governor of Arizona.

# CLOSE-UPS

---□---

*You can't use tact with a congressman! A congressman is a hog!*
*You must take a stick and hit him on the snout!*

*-- Unidentified cabinet officer, 1869, to Henry Adams*

Woe to the squeamish and weak-kneed who gazed upon the Senate floor during the 19th century. Charles Dickens visited in 1842 and warned: "The state to which these carpets are reduced by the universal disregard of the spittoon, with which every honorable member is accommodated ...... do not admit of being described. I strongly recommend all strangers not to look at the floor; and if they happen to drop anything, though it be their purse, not to pick it up with an ungloved hand on any account." Modern polished brass spittoons are still in place at the foot of several senators' desks. However, they are there merely for decorative purposes and as reminders of the past. Less well-known is that each is stamped at the base: *Made in Taiwan*.

*John Adams*

For the first few weeks of its existence the patrician Senate spent much of its time trying to agree on titles for the country's new leaders. Vice President John Adams, presiding, wanted fine titles to reflect the majesty and elevation of high office. He scorned a suggestion to call George Washington *President of the United States*, scoffing that even fire companies and cricket clubs had their own presidents. After rejecting His *Elective Majesty* the Senate settled on *His Highness, the President of the United States of America, and Protector of their Liberties*. Members of the House of Representatives would have none of such pomposity and stood their ground until the full Congress abided by the simple title of *President*. Adams had been so eager for titles that his colleagues playfully dubbed him *His Rotundity*. Others suggested he be called *His Superfluous Excellency*.

Lamb's Biographical Dictionary of the U.S.

*Minority Leader William Knowland was having a hard time hearing Sen. Strom Thurmond and was afraid he might miss his cue if the South Carolinian sprang a surprise motion. "I do not want him to strain his voice," said Knowland, "but I should like him to speak a little louder." Thurmond invited the California Republican to move in closer. Knowland wouldn't budge, "this happening to be my seat as the minority leader." Thurmond persisted, claiming "There is an excellent seat here." Not according to Knowland. "I am very well satisfied with the seat to which I am assigned," he repeated. Thurmond got the message, raised his voice a fraction and moved on to complete his record-breaking filibuster of more than 24 hours.*

Rep. Robert Rich got a huge round of applause from the public galleries when he said the House of Representatives had urgent need of a psychiatrist. This was the Pennsylvania Republican's reaction to his perception of a crackpot bill in 1950 allowing the government to pay freight costs of surplus food bought to support farm prices. In his opinion Congress had finally gone too far. It had forced up the price of food so much that many Americans could no longer buy it. Rich's peers remained unimpressed. They voted for the legislation.

*So many congressmen flocked to a horserace worth $20,000 in prize money that the House of Representatives had to shut down for lack of a quorum. It happened on a spring day in 1838 when the House was forced to adjourn in mid-afternoon. The horses were not the only attraction at the racecourse. Gambling tables were set up for roulette and faro and liquor was plentiful. John Fairfield (D-Me.) was among the few representatives who spurned the races in favor of legislative business. Angered by the low turnout which ruined his day, Fairfield wrote his wife, "It is a foul stain upon the character of an American Congress."*

Not every member of Congress came to Washington for the common good. A late 19th century representative from the South confided to a reporter covering Congress that he ran for election only to make enough money out of the government to buy himself a fine farm. By all measures he succeeded handsomely. The congressman served four years in the capital, taking back more than $18,000 in savings from a total four-year pay of $21,500. "I paid about $1500 to the campaign committees and the other $2000 went for my Washington expenses." He said he had lived in a comfortable Washington boarding house for $35 a month. This included laundry and "fare as good as I had at home."

When midnight struck in the House of Representatives on March 3, 1835 members argued for almost four more hours whether they were entitled to vote or whether the congressional term had expired. Rep. George Briggs reminded them that none other than Rep. John Quincy Adams, a former president, had said a few days earlier that on March 3 the House would be numbered with the dead. "But here we are on the 4th of March," said Briggs, "and if we are dead, we are the most noisy dead I have ever heard of." The lawmakers went home at 3.30 a.m., without solving the issue, after they discovered the Senate had already quit and gone home.

*All manner of luxuries and other indulgences were charged up to congressmen's stationery accounts in the 19th century. The disguised office supplies included bottles of perfume, kid gloves, bear's grease to apply to the hair, razors, scissors, pen knives, pocketbooks and swichell - a beverage supposedly containing French brandy and Jamaica rum. These and other items were requested whenever a government official went up to New York to buy "stationery supplies."*

## BEAUTIES OF THE FRANKING PRIVILEGE.

MEMBER OF CONGRESS, *soliloquizing.* "Seven cotton shirts, three flannel, six pairs of socks, one collar, five pocket-handkerchiefs, three pair of drawers, two linen coats—that's all, I guess; and as the mail's just closing, that must do for to-day."

[Mails his clothes-bag under his frank, and has his linen cheaply washed at home in Wisconsin.]

*Congressmen used to mail their dirty laundry home free of charge*

Exasperated U.S. Postmasters reached breaking point over free mailing privileges for congressmen when legislators began sending their dirty clothing to be laundered more cheaply in their home towns. The franking privilege required only the congressman's signature instead of a postage stamp. Some congressmen had so corrupted the system that they were shipping entire barrels of china at taxpayers' expense. By 1869 an estimated ton of free mail was being sent out of the Washington, D.C. post office. The Postmaster General, already running his department in the red, demanded that the "evil" abuse of privilege come to an end. By 1873 public scorn was so widespread that Congress was forced to abolish the privilege. But the very next year Congress began hauling back its franking rights so that, by 1891 it had restored everything formerly surrendered.

Humphrey Marshall was not alone among congressmen who gambled away fortunes at Pendleton's Palace of Fortune on Pennsylvania Avenue, but he surely suffered the most undignified loss. The Representative from Kentucky had already resigned from Congress in 1852 to accept an appointment as Minister to China when he lost the diplomatic shirt on his back. He had wagered his formal diplomatic uniform and six months future pay when his luck ran out. Pendleton himself stepped in to rescue the red-faced Marshall. He loaned the Minister-designate enough money to get to China. When Marshall returned two years later his reputation was unsullied. Twice more he was elected to Congress.

---

*Unpunctual congressmen made George Washington wait more than a month to learn that he had been elected President of the United States. The first Congress was scheduled to meet on Wednesday, March 4, 1789 in New York City's Federal Hall. Cannons boomed and church bells peeled ceremonially but only 8 of the 22 senators and 13 of the 59 representatives arrived for business. A scribe with a meticulously neat handwriting noted in the Senate Journal: The number not being sufficient to constitute a quorum, they adjourned.*

*On April Fool's Day the House of Representatives finally had a quorum but sufficient numbers of senators did not assemble until April 6. Representatives walked upstairs to the Senate chamber to watch John Langdon, newly-elected president pro tempore of the Senate, count the electoral votes. Then he announced that George Washington had won with 69 votes. John Adams, runner-up with 34 votes, was declared the new nation's vice president.*

*Rumors flew thick and fast in Washington during World War 11, as Rep. Clare Boothe Luce (R-Conn.) learned to her dismay. When she joked about writing a play on Congress tattlers spread the word that she was serious, forcing her into a public denial. Interest peaked when rumor-mongers gave details about one scene considered by Luce, author of the sellout plays* The Women *and* Kiss the Boys Good-By. *It had freshmen representatives coming upon a reclining colleague. They thought he was asleep on the couch when actually he had passed away three years earlier.*

The frail sensibilities of British writer Frances Trollope were shaken to the core when she visited the House of Representatives in 1824. True, she was highly impressed with the House chamber which she found to be a splendid hall fitted up in a stately and sumptuous manner. But she was profoundly upset by the conduct of the congressmen. She promptly let the world know about it in her book, *Domestic Manners of the Americans.* Trollope described the representatives "sitting in the most unseemly attitudes, a large majority with their hats on, and nearly all spitting to an excess that decency forbids me to describe."

*Railroads brought prosperity to the country but sorrow to many a congressman. The steam engines put an end to the wild gambling ways of legislators because they could no longer indulge out of sight of their wives and children. The long and slow stage-coach journeys which had forced congressional families to live apart became a thing of the past. Women and children no longer had to remain in their home states while congressmen traveled alone to Washington for legislative sessions. The railways brought families within quick and easy reach of each other. And so, many congressmen who had been members of gambling "messes" in private boarding houses, were forced to move out, give up their profligate ways and move in with their wives and children.*

*German immigrant writer Francis Grund couldn't believe his eyes when he first visited Washington in the 1830s. There seemed to be so many idle dandies walking the streets. "Washington," he wrote, "is a city of American idlers - a set of gentlemen of such peculiar merit. They live in what is called elegant style, rise in the morning at eight or nine, have breakfast in their own rooms, then smoke five or six cigars until twelve, at which time they dress for the Senate; few gentlemen ever honoring the House of Representatives with their presence." Grund, who later became an American citizen and U.S. consul in Europe, continued, "The Senate is, indeed, the finest drawing-room in Washington; for it is there the young women of fashion resort for the purpose of exhibiting their attractions. The Capitol is, in point of fashion, the opera-house of the city; the House of Representatives being the crush-room. In the absence of a decent theatre, the Capitol furnishes a tolerable place of rendezvous."*

There was nothing stiffly Victorian about the late 19th century Congress. Senators thirsting for a swig of alcohol used to clap their hands to summon a page. Then they ordered cold tea - the euphemism for any kind of alcohol - from the restaurant below. They kept a sense of decorum in the cloakrooms, drinking only from small bottles of private supplies stored in restrooms leading off the main vestibule.

*When three important government buildings went up in flames shortly before Thomas Jefferson took over the presidency from John Adams, a suspicious congressman hinted at arson to destroy state secrets. The fires destroyed records in the Treasury, the War office and at a federal arms factory. Representative John Fowler rushed off a letter to his "Fellow Citizens" in Kentucky. "These fires thus succeeding each other, at a period when patronage and the secrets of office were about to be transferred to different hands, could not but excite the worst suspicions; after much enquiry on the subject, the only thing discovered is that nobody knows anything about the origin of the fires!"*

# HIGH DRAMA

---□---

*A speech is entertaining only when serenely
detached from all information.*

*-- Sen. Henry Ashurst (R-Ariz.) 1939*

Kentucky's Sen. Henry Clay startled his colleagues during the historic debate on slavery in 1850 when he held up a fragment of George Washington's mahogany coffin. It had been given to him that morning by a man who felt Clay would treasure the precious relic. Clay used it for dramatic effect to warn senators that failure to support his call for a compromise between Northern free states and Southern slave states might lead to the destruction of the Union. Holding aloft the macabre memento he said it had been given to him "as a warning voice, coming from the grave to the Congress now in session to beware, to pause, to reflect before they lend themelves to any purposes which shall destroy that Union which was cemented by his (Washington's) exertions and example." The relic apparently made an impression. Congress agreed to the celebrated Compromise of 1850, which helped fend off the Civil War by 11 years.

*An impassioned Rep. John Taber (R-N.Y.) roared so loudly into the microphone during a House debate that the amplified sound cured the lifelong deafness of Rep. Leonard Schuetz (D-Ill.). Schuetz, owner of a construction company, was at first so dazed by the sound waves that he tottered out to the cloakroom and collapsed on a sofa "feeling goofy." Though he could hear reasonably well in his right ear, he had been totally deaf in the other since birth. As Schuetz tried to recover his equilibrium in that memorable spring of 1940, a colleague opened the connecting door to the House chamber and another blast of Taber's voice hit home. Moments later Schuetz returned to the chamber. Only then did he realize that his hearing had been fully restored in both ears.*

When the Queen of England visited the Capitol during the Bicentennial celebrations she was conducted down the steps to her car by Nordy Hoffman, Senate sergeant-at-arms. "Your Royal Highness, we're so happy that you came," he said with deep admiration. "Thank you," she replied as she climbed into her limousine. Hoffman backed off and was preparing to leave when the Queen stepped out of her car. "Mr. Hoffman," she said to his astonishment, "I have never had a welcome like this any place I've ever been. Thank you."

*The 1988 session of Congress was dragging on interminably for the likes of Sen. James McClure (R-Idaho). By late October he could take no more of it. He stood up in the Senate chamber and by way of protest quoted Oliver Cromwell's snappy rebuke in 1653 to British parliamentarians. "You have sat too long here for any good you have been doing. Depart, I say, and let us have done with you. In the name of God, go!"*

There was a breathtaking interlude during humdrum debate on Capitol Hill when a grinning President Truman walked uninvited into the Senate chamber and sat down at his former desk. It happened in the summer of 1947 after he lunched in the Capitol with a handful of senators who dared him to do it to see what would happen. Senate president pro tempore Arthur Vandenberg (R-Mich.) was so taken aback that as he wriggled for a suitable reaction he announced there was no precedent for what Harry Truman had just done. Vandenberg then made history himself by violating the rule enabling only an incumbent senator to speak from the floor. "The ex-senator from Missouri is recognized for five minutes," he said.

Truman stood up with an impish smile and said he was happy he had taken up the dare of those he had lunched with. "I sometimes get homesick for this seat," he added. "I spent what I think were the best 10 years of my life in the Senate." Vandenberg didn't even try and call for order as spectators in the galleries joined the legislators in wild applause. The beaming president waved to everyone as he strode out delighted with himself.

The galleries were thronged to capacity, the welcome was tumultuous and Speaker Sam Rayburn called him "one of the most distinguished figures on earth" when British premier Winston Churchill addressed a joint meeting of Congress in 1943. But a legless soldier in a wheelchair at the back of the House chamber captured the imagination of observers. Lt. Hon. Richard Wood, son of British Ambassador Lord Halifax, had lost both his legs in the Tripoli campaign. The khaki-uniformed young Briton, honored for his bravery, was allowed onto the House floor to fulfill a simple wish of wanting to see and hear the great wartime leader give another stirring oration.

*When a spectator in the Senate gallery decided he wanted to take part in debate on post World War 11 international relief he stood up and shouted, "Mr. president, will the senator yield for a speaker in the gallery?" Shocked by the disturbance, senators swiveled their heads towards the galleries as the presiding officer, Sen. Raymond Baldwin (R-Conn.) called for order. Unlike senators, the man did not wait for permission to continue speaking and had to be forcibly removed by four guards as he kicked and screamed. When he was out of sight and earshot senators resumed their dignified debate.*

When the first blind senator lost his bid for reelection in 1921 he predicted in writing that he would return to Congress in 1931, then wedged the note into a crack in his Senate desk. The first thing Thomas Gore (D-Okla.) did on being reelected in 1931 was to retrieve the forecast from his desk. Gore was only eight when a stick thrown by a playmate blinded him in one eye. Three years later he lost his other eye in an accidental firing of a toy gun. Despite the handicap he became a lawyer and, as a colleague noted, one of the world's greatest orators. When Oklahoma was admitted to the Union, Gore, 37, was the youngest member of the Senate. He had a phenomenal memory, being able to recite the names of every senator when he was only 16. His own library numbered 50,000 books, which he read with the help of his wife, secretary and friends. Gore told time by pressing a button on his wristwatch and then listening to the tell-tale sounds of the correct hour and minute.

Three men singled out to hold the office of President of the United States walked together in procession in the House of Representatives on January 14, 1969. As President Richard Nixon appeared to deliver his first State of the Union address, he was escorted into the chamber by Gerald Ford (R-Mich.) and George Bush (R-Tex.). The two congressmen who later occupied the White House were among a group of nine representatives appointed by the House Speaker for the high honor that day.

The birth of a baby girl in Los Angeles, California at 3.55 p.m. on Friday, November 23, 1973 set off a flurry of excitement on Capitol Hill. It was the first time in history that a member of Congress had given birth. The mother, Yvonne Burke, (D-Calif.), had three weeks earlier been granted an unprecedented maternity leave of absence from the House of Representatives. Burke, 41, named her 7 lb. 9 oz. daughter Autumn Roxann.

*The Capitol had not witnessed anything like it in almost half a century when the sergeant-at-arms and a posse of police forcibly dragged a senator from his office onto the Senate chamber to make up a quorum. Sen. Robert Packwood (R-Ore.) tried hiding out in his office, with a chair blocking one door, but Sergeant-at-Arms Henry Giugni slipped in by unlocking another door with a skeleton key. Republicans had scattered in hopes of forcing adjournment, through lack of a quorum, on a campaign spending limits bill they opposed. Righteous Democrats defended their instructions to force arrest of the absent Republicans. "Senators are supposed to be grown-up people, not kids," said Majority Leader Robert Byrd (D-W. Va.). Not so, countered Sen. Arlen Specter (R-Pa.). "The knock on the door and the forceful entry smack of Nazi Germany." Packwood made light of it all, suffering nothing more than a bruised finger.*

When Sen. Wayne Morse (Ind-Ore.) rose to filibuster during debate on the 1954 atomic energy bill another senator wisecracked, "Now we can all go to bed." True to form, Morse spoke for six hours and 13 minutes. When he began he held out some hope that he would not drone on for 22 hours as he had done the year before. He wore a red rose in his lapel and said he would talk until it wilted. But as if to give him encouragement, three more red roses were delivered to his desk during the night. When the Senate finally recessed for a Sunday break it had sat in almost continuous session for 85 hours and 48 minutes. The toll was just as heavy on weary staff. One of the official scribes wilted and was carried out on a stretcher.

*A lively 19th century scene in the House of Representatives*

John Calhoun

*S*outh Carolina's most famous senator, John Calhoun, wanted to refuse the $500,000 gift from an Englishman to found the Smithsonian Institution. "It is beneath the dignity of the United States to receive presents of this kind from anyone," he scolded senators in 1836. In any case, Calhoun argued, the federal government had no right to the money because the purpose for which it was intended, education, was controlled by the states. It reminded him of the gift of a statue of Thomas Jefferson in the Rotunda of the Capitol. Every time Calhoun passed it he said he felt "outraged" because it had been put there without the consent of Congress. "We accepted a statue of Mr. Jefferson which is no more like him than I am, and we made a tacit admission, by its acceptance, that we were too stingy to purchase one worthy of the man and of the nation. And now what would we do by this? We would accept a donation from a foreigner to do with it what we have no right to do, and just as if we were not rich enough ourselves to do what is proposed, or too mean to do it if it were in our power."

The four Puerto Rican nationalists who went on a shooting rampage in the House of Representatives in 1954 meant to attack the Senate but they got lost inside the labyrinthine Capitol. The three men and a woman had taken an elevator in the basement of the Senate wing. As they got off on the main floor they asked others in the elevator how to get to the Senate gallery. Dr. Grover Ensley, staff director of Congress' over-all Joint Economic Committee, gave them precise directions. They never made it to the Senate. However, within an hour they opened fire from a gallery in the House, wounding five congressmen. When Ensley heard three had been captured he told police he had ridden the elevator with four Puerto Ricans. Soon afterwards police detained the fourth would-be assassin.

———————☐———————

*Newsmen presented Vice President Charles Dawes with a 4 ft. high alarm clock to remind him of the day he missed what would have been a rare tie-breaking vote and sank the confirmation of a cabinet officer. New to the job, Dawes had been presiding officer of the Senate only a few days when it held confirmation hearings for Charles Warren to be Attorney General in the administration of Calvin Coolidge. Six senators were lined up to speak as the day's session drew to a close and both the majority and minority leaders told Dawes a vote would not be taken that day. Acting on this information, the inexperienced Dawes left the Capitol. Almost immediately, however, five of the six scheduled speakers dropped out, forcing an early vote. When the Senate split down the middle it gave the vice president his only constitutional opportunity to vote in the Senate. Dawes would have carried the day but he was nowhere to be found. As a result the confirmation was voted down and Warren did not become Attorney General.*

*It took 159 years before a female minister offered the daily prayer in the House of Representatives and when Rev. Annalee Stewart rose she called for an end to weapons of war. The ordained Methodist minister prayed for God to "take from our frightened hands the bomb and bayonet." Speaking just three years after World War 11, she decried "so much fear, suspicion and planning for the destruction of mankind."*

———□———

The 53rd Congress was memorably dramatic for the two military veterans who hobbled on crutches, each having lost a leg in the Civil War. Daniel Sickles (D-N.Y.) had risen to the rank of major general in the Union Army. William Stone (D-Ky.) had fought as a captain with the Confederates. Whenever a vote was taken Sickles and Stone remained seated. Congressmen asked them how they wished to vote then took a crutch from each amputee. As the congressmen passed between the tellers they made a show of holding the crutches while pronouncing the voting intentions of each man.

For months chairman William Fulbright of the Senate Foreign Relations Committee had been trying to get Secretary of State Henry Kissinger to hearings on detente with the Soviets. Kissinger always pleaded an overloaded work schedule. Finally Fulbright's staff director nailed him down to appear in August 1974. But a day or two before, a Kissinger aide telephoned to say his boss had no time to prepare a proper statement. The staff director exploded, "We won't take that as an excuse." The aide paused. "Well don't you dare tell anybody, but I think there's something brewing at the White House and maybe the committee won't want to have a hearing that day anyway." The director reported to Fulbright that Kissinger had backed out again. "Well, I'm not surprised," said Fulbright. "I think the president's about to resign." On August 9 Richard Nixon resigned.

———□———

Congressmen speaking sympathetically of the South during the Civil War did so at their peril. In 1864 Rep. Benjamin Harris (D-Md.) told Congress, "The South asked you to let them live in peace. But no; you said you would bring them into subjection. I hope that you will never subjugate the South." Stung by his "treasonable language and a gross contempt of the House," representatives failed to boot him out of Congress because they lacked a two thirds majority. But they ganged up to censure Harris with a 98-20 vote declaring him "an unworthy member of the House." The following year a military court convicted him of harboring two paroled Confederate soldiers. He got a three year prison term and a lifetime ban on federal government employment.

**Senate rules against the admission of animals to the galleries caved in when a blind woman refused to take no for an answer in 1950. Anita Blair, 28, a free-lance lecturer, told sergeant-at-arms Joseph Duke that she had come all the way from Chicago with her German shepherd and would not be turned back. The sergeant-at-arms relented - but he ordered a guard and a detective to keep an eye on the dog, just in case it was not as tame as it looked.**

Sen. Leverett Saltonstall, a former Republican governor of Massachusetts, vividly remembered April 12, 1945. He was one of the few members on the Senate floor listening to a speech while Vice President Harry Truman presided. A page walked over and handed a pink slip to Saltonstall. It was a note from Truman. "Governor, I want to go out and into my room to meet a Missouri soldier boy. Will you come up here and sit in this seat?" Saltonstall stood in until Truman returned an hour and a half later. Shortly afterwards Truman recessed the Senate. Within an hour he received a call to go to the White House. Franklin Roosevelt had died. Truman was the new president.

A sober senator swore he saw a marble table move a foot across the same room in which Daniel Webster stored his private casks of wine more than a century earlier. Sen. Patrick Leahy (D-Vt.) acquired the historic hideaway in the Capitol in 1984 and spruced it up with fresh coats of paint and new furniture. Soon after, he watched incredulously as the 150 lb. marble table vibrated and moved while everything else remained in place. Leahy confessed "it scared the hell out of me." Since then the eerie scene repeated itself a number of times. Leahy dedicated his hideaway *The Daniel Webster Memorial Room* and even issued a party invitation to the great 19th century Massachusetts orator. But no one reported seeing Webster's ghostly presence.

William Mailliard was mighty proud when his congresswoman came out of the House chamber in 1934 to greet him but he blushed crimson when she boomed in the presence of 40 bystanders, "Your grandfather was the handsomest man I ever met. But for the grace of God I might have been your grandmother!" No one had briefed Mailliard, 17, about Rep. Florence Kahn's legendary voice. The California Republican was so loud that when told the House was installing a public address system, President Franklin Roosevelt had quipped, "Why? I can hear Florence Kahn from here without it." Mailliard's meeting with Kahn echoed down the decades in more ways than one. The man who defeated her in 1936 was himself ousted 16 years later by Mailliard.

Sen. John Eaton's 1829 marriage to Peggy O'Neill, a flirtatious beauty queen and innkeeper's daughter, so scandalized Washington society women that the government fell apart. President Andrew Jackson ousted three cabinet members because they refused to order their wives to stop snubbing Peggy. She was only a teen-ager when Jackson and Eaton, both U.S. Senators from Tennessee, first lodged at O'Neill's tavern in downtown Washington. Peggy married a navy purser, but after his suicide she married Eaton, by then Secretary of War in President Jackson's cabinet. Jackson remained so loyal to the newlyweds that he boycotted his church when the pastor accused Eaton and Peggy of adultery before their marriage. Two years after the scandal broke Eaton quit the government to become Governor of Florida and then Minister to Spain. Peggy continued to shock society after his death. At the age of 60 she married a 20-year-old music teacher, who later eloped with her granddaughter. Peggy lived another 23 years, passing away in 1879. The women who shunned her would have envied Peggy's daughters. One married Austrian Baron Rothschild and another wedded a French Duke.

*Four-month-old Ralph Coar, Jr. made history in 1940 when he became the first person baptized in the chamber of the House of Representatives. The baby boy was granted the unique honor because his father was head of the House radio room. To complete the family circle, the ceremony was performed by the baby's grandfather, a Massachusetts pastor.*

When Constantino Brumidi died penniless Congress paid for his funeral because he had done such a good job decorating the Capitol's walls and ceilings. "He died poor, without money enough to bury his worn-out body," said Sen. Daniel Voorhees (D-Ind.) "but how rich the inheritance he has left to the present and succeeding ages ...... creations of imperishable beauty wherever his touch has been!"   Five months before, the 74-year-old Italian immigrant artist almost plunged 58 ft. to the floor of the Rotunda. He dangled by his arms from a ladder for 15 minutes when his chair overturned on scaffolding. Seventy years after his death in 1880, Congress placed a bronze marker over his grave. His bust has a place of honor in the Brumidi Corridor of the Senate wing.

Congressmen have always seemed aghast when information known only to them has frequently found its way into the media. On one such occasion during the 19th century senators were perplexed when much of what they said and did in executive session appeared in the newspapers the following day. As senators pondered the source of the leak one of their number, Sen. James Green (D-Mo.) summoned a Senate employee to his desk. He confided that he had seen someone in the gallery and asked the man to investigate. The employee quickly spied a large black cat in the gallery but it instantly disappeared through an open trap door. He reported his findings to the Missourian. The following morning Green rose to tell his colleagues that he had discovered how news of the executive sessions was reaching the general public. The intruder had been found. It was, he said to uproarious laughter, a large black cat. The leaks continued - even though the cat disappeared forever several weeks later.

*Dixon Hall Lewis weighed over 400 lbs.*

So many people tried to catch a glimpse of Daniel Webster during a momentous speech in 1830 that they pushed the 400 lb. bulk of Rep. Dixon Hall Lewis against painted glass partitioning the lobby from the Senate chamber. The fattest member of Congress was just as determined to get a peek at Webster. He pulled out his penknife and began scratching the paint off the glass. The high-pitched scrapping distracted a lot of people but no one could pinpoint where it was coming from. Lewis himself suffered from the exertions in his cramped position but it was worth it. When the wide-girthed Alabaman had scratched a peep-hole as large as his hand he had an enviable view of Webster.

Sen. Wayne Morse sprang an unwelcome surprise on President Kennedy during a telephone call from Capitol Hill to the White House. The maverick Morse (Ind.-Ore.) was chairman of Senate conferees considering a higher education bill when he placed the call to get clarification on the president's intentions. Morse spoke from a telephone booth but was overheard by bystanders because he left the door open. When he'd finished the business at hand, Morse, an early opponent of U.S. involvement in Vietnam, raised his voice to a shout as he told the president, "Well, Jack, since I've got you on the phone I want to tell you that you better get the hell out of Vietnam. You're going down in a pit there!" Kennedy was overheard shouting back but only Morse knew what the president said, and he wasn't telling.

**Betty Richmond thought the congressmen were talking drivel so she gave them a mouthful from the public gallery. "You can go on like you are for a million years and you won't end the depression!" she shouted in 1933. "You don't spend money you haven't got!" Capitol police did not bother to arrest the well-dressed woman who, having had her say, immediately got up and stormed out in disgust.**

*Spectators rush into the impeachment trial of President Andrew Johnson in 1868*

President Andrew Johnson got 20 complimentary entrance tickets to hand out to friends wanting to view his own impeachment trial. The limited number of tickets were the hottest item in Washington during the historic trial by the Senate. Printed with the date and signature of the sergeant-at-arms, they admitted bearers to the cramped public galleries. Only 1000 were run off the press and the colors changed daily to outwit counterfeiters and scalpers. A large quantity of the coveted paper slips were handed out to the city's social and political elite, including 40 to the diplomatic corps, four each to the chief justice, speaker of the House and each senator, and two for each house member, supreme

In 1875 Congress passed a special bill allowing General William Tecumseh Sherman's daughter to receive, duty free, a $300,000 diamond necklace wedding gift from the Khedive of Egypt. The extraordinary bill relieved young Minnie Sherman and her bridegroom, Thomas Fitch, from paying $75,000 in duties. The legislation was also necessary because Fitch, an engineer in the U.S. Navy, could not otherwise have accepted the present. However, the bride got to keep only a quarter of the jewelry. Minnie's mother ordered the diamonds re-set into brooches and earrings for each of her four daughters. Her reasoning? The extravagant gift was really the Khedive's way of saying thank you to the general for military advice.

---

*The globe-trotting congressional delegation arrived in Athens pooped out, ready to sup at 6 p.m. and then hit the sack. Trouble was the U.S. ambassador had organized a party at 8 p.m. to meet with the city's governing and social elite. None of the visitors felt like a party and told the ambassador they wouldn't attend. Embarrassed and hoping for a face-saving excuse for the Greeks, the ambassador was saved by the tragic sinking of a ship off Piraeus that night with loss of life. Authorities declared a period of mourning and the ambassador was able to call off the party without getting egg on his face.*

*A Meeting of the Committee on Irrigation*

A filibuster failed in the Senate in 1908 because one of the participating senators was blind. The lead part was taken by Sen. Robert La Follette (R-Wis.) who managed to keep speaking for more than 18 hours by drinking a concoction of egg and milk. By prearrangement, he was succeeded by the blind Sen. Thomas Gore (D-Okla.), who was scheduled to hold the floor until relieved by Sen. William Stone of Missouri. Gore stopped talking in the mistaken belief that Stone was in the chamber and ready to take over. Seizing the opportunity, Sen. Nelson Aldrich (R-R.I.) promptly put his motion and as his name was on the top of the roll he voted immediately his name was called. This effectively squelched any hopes the filibusterers had of resuming their waffle.

Few men in the history of Congress commanded as much respect from their colleagues as Sen. Daniel Webster of Massachusetts. Once he was taken ill on his way down to Washington, D.C. and had to stop over in New York to recover. It was nothing serious but word reached the Capitol that Webster was dangerously ill. A day or two later he resumed his journey. When Webster entered the Senate chamber the effect was electric. Every senator stood up spontaneously and normal business resumed only after the great orator had taken his seat.

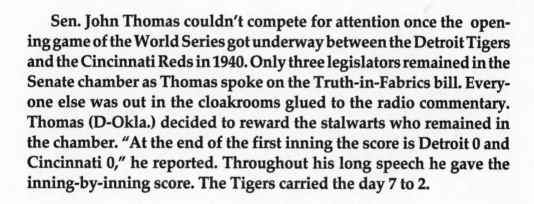

Sen. John Thomas couldn't compete for attention once the opening game of the World Series got underway between the Detroit Tigers and the Cincinnati Reds in 1940. Only three legislators remained in the Senate chamber as Thomas spoke on the Truth-in-Fabrics bill. Everyone else was out in the cloakrooms glued to the radio commentary. Thomas (D-Okla.) decided to reward the stalwarts who remained in the chamber. "At the end of the first inning the score is Detroit 0 and Cincinnati 0," he reported. Throughout his long speech he gave the inning-by-inning score. The Tigers carried the day 7 to 2.

# CAPITOL HILL STAFF

□

*When Congress will rise no mortal can tell:*
*not from the quantity but dilatoriness of business.*

*--Thomas Jefferson, Letter to daughter, Mary, November 27, 1803*

The Japanese man was lost in the Capitol as he tried to find then Sen. Richard Nixon's private hideaway. "You're in the wrong building," said Capitol policeman Leonard Ballard. "He's in the Senate office building." The Japanese man persisted. "I have an appointment to have breakfast with him in his office in the Capitol." Ballard realized the man was telling the truth because Nixon did have breakfasts in his hideaway. They went down the corridor to room 236. "Come in," said Nixon (R-Calif.). Then, addressing Ballard, the future president said, "You will probably enjoy meeting this man. He is now a Baptist minister in California but he is the captain who led the raid on Pearl Harbor." Instantly, Ballard asked for the man's autograph. The former enemy obliged, writing his name in both English and Japanese then adding a biblical reference: Luke 23:34. Back home, Ballard opened his Bible. It read, "Father, forgive them; for they know not what they do."

In all her 20 years in Congress Rep. Edith Green (D-Ore.) refused to play second fiddle because of her gender. But others were not so independent. One day she got the signed backing for a particular issue from every female member of Congress. Then suddenly she got a call from the office of one of the women signatories, a West Virginian. It was the legislator's son, who also acted as his mother's administrative assistant. He asked for removal of his mother's name from the letter. "Why?" asked Green dumbfounded. "In the South we like our women to be quiet," the man replied. Green wanted to talk it over with the congresswoman but was told she was not in.

The House of Representatives chaplain probably wondered about the power of prayer when he read that his annual salary was $3,750,000. It didn't take long to bring him down to earth. There were too many zeros in the official report of the Appropriations Committee in 1949. When the typographical error was corrected the chaplain's pay was reported as a humble $3,750 a year.

*A message from the President of the United States*

Any time the doorkeeper appeared ceremoniously in the Senate aisle proclaiming, "A message from the President of the United States!", young pages jostled for positions near the waste basket. All of them, during World War 1, were eager to retrieve the official presidential seal from the castaway envelope. With great formality, the vice president would recognize the doorkeeper and bid him come forward. The sealed message would be handed first to the clerk and then to the vice president. After it was opened the pages scrambled with practiced decorum for the rare souvenir.

*James Buchanan*

Though used to waiting hand and foot upon the high and the mighty, many congressional pages experienced what one of them called "the golden moment" of life. Christian Eckloff's came in the mid-19th century when Sen. William Bigler (D-Pa.) asked the teenager to deliver a letter personally to President James Buchanan. Eckloff took the horse-drawn omnibus from Capitol Hill along Pennsylvania Avenue, intending to get off at the White House. But with two blocks to go he spotted the president walking on the sidewalk in front of fashionable Willard's Hotel. He jumped off the 'bus, took off his hat and approached the chief executive. "Mr. Buchanan, I have been directed by senator Bigler to give you this letter in person." The bachelor president smiled and opened the envelope as Eckloff stood perfectly still, "scarcely daring to breathe in the august presence." When he had read the letter, Buchanan, who was longsighted in one eye and short-sighted in the other, looked down at the page, remarking, "No answer." Eckloff, beside himself with excitement, hopped on the next 'bus back to the Capitol.

A confidential British embassy run-down on every member of the elite Senate Foreign Relations Committee dropped out of the pocket of visiting Prime Minister Harold Macmillan and was secretly copied by a committee staffer before it was returned. The spectacular coup revealed that the British had a low or critical opinion of everyone except chairman William Fulbright, a Rhodes Scholar. The embassy even had less than flattering words about Sen. Alexander Wiley (R-Wis.) married to a Briton. The secret document dropped to the floor during an official lunch with the committee. When Macmillan left, committee clerk Darrell St. Claire scooped it up. Later St. Claire went to the Senate chamber and spoke to long-time staff director Carl Marcy while the British leader addressed legislators. "You'd better give this back to the prime minister," said St. Claire, explaining what it was. "The PM dropped it when he was at lunch. When he left, I picked it up." Marcy dutifully returned the purloined piece of paper. Then he asked St. Claire, "Well, did you make a copy of it?" Replied the clerk: "Of course!"

---

A typist's error almost led to an innocent man's arrest by order of Sen. Joe McCarthy (R-Wis.) during his heyday as chairman of the Permanent Subcommittee on Investigations. Chief clerk Ruth Watt had typed up a subpoena for the man to appear on Capitol Hill at 10. Red-faced, she realized her error when bewildered police called late at night to say the witness was in the empty building waiting to testify. Watt had typed out p.m. instead of a.m. The witness was blissfully unaware how his absence was felt at the morning meeting. When he failed to appear, the fearsome McCarthy had snarled, "I guess we'll have to have a meeting and cite him for contempt."

**H**awaiian Night was planned as an innocent evening of cultural entertainment by a group of congressional secretaries styling themselves The Little Congress. They had even arranged with Hawaii's Republican Delegate, Samuel King, to have a hula dancer and an Hawaiian orchestra. Unfortunately, they made the mistake of scheduling the event inside the House Office Building. When Speaker Joe Byrns got word of the planned party he immediately issued a ban on the hula dance. In a sign of the times - 1935 - he thought it "unwise to convert a House caucus room into a dance hall."

*There was much mirth inside the Capitol when Senate pages played an April Fool's joke on Sen. John Sherman, a Republican notorious for his miserly ways. The youngsters placed a wallet on the floor just outside the Senate chamber, attached a length of thread to it and scurried into an adjacent room. As Sherman came by and stooped to pick up the wallet, the boys tugged on the thread and hauled the money out of the senator's reach. Sherman, an Ohioan who later became Secretary of the Treasury, indignantly reported the incident to the pages' supervisor. They kept their jobs but wound up with a severe rebuke from the sergeant-at-arms.*

Many a floor reporter for the Congressional Record has the gentlemanly ways of Sen. Hugh Scott to thank for bailing them out of tight spots. Republican Scott was a connoisseur of Chinese art and culture. Occasionally, when he inserted a Chinese language expression into one of his speeches, the floor reporter would stall and utter a silent cry for help. Scott always obliged. The courtly, bespectacled Pennsylvanian would walk over to the flustered reporter and smilingly hand over a note with the expression written out.

The Senate had its own Wailing Wall in the early 1950s. That was how clerk Darrell St. Claire characterized the Rules and Administration Committee because so many people came to him pleading for help and special favors. Senators' aides wanted more office space. They cried out for more new-fangled typewriters. They begged permission to spend more on constituent mailings. In retirement after almost four decades on the Hill, St. Claire confessed how he handled it. He made "lying promises," knowing he would never be able to keep them. "I must have told at least 50 lies a day on the telephone," said St. Claire, who rose to become assistant secretary of the Senate.

**P**ity the overworked Senate reporters and transcribers. In 1949 they proved that senators gab more than representatives. Five hundred hours more in that single year. That translated into four months extra work in man-hours. Wearily, they took their case to the Senate Rules Committee, pleading for more man-power. Senators didn't take long to talk the matter over. They quickly hired one more reporter and an extra transcriber.

E. Ross Adair's election to Congress had a lot to do with the happy-go-lucky Capitol police force in the 1930s. It gave the young Adair time to study law all the while he should have been working as a part-time policeman. Given the graveyard shift from midnight to 8 a.m., he was told to stand guard at the main entrance to the old Senate Office Building. The quiet location suited the young George Washington University Law School student fine. When Adair, from Indiana, reported for duty he carried a typewriter in one hand and law books in the other. If given a daytime police assignment, he grumbled how it interferred with his studies. Adair's superiors obviously expected things to remain quiet on the Hill. They gave him a .32 calibre pistol but didn't think it necessary to give him any training. "Use it if you have to," they said.

An Illinois family visiting Washington was barred by the Secret Service from entering the cathedral because President Lyndon Johnson's daughter was about to be married inside. When the visitors got to the White House they found it closed for the same reason. On their way to Mt. Vernon they got caught up in a traffic jam and arrived to find the gates already closed for the night. The following day they lined up for admission to the Senate galleries but were told by Capitol Hill policeman Leonard Ballard that the Senate had just adjourned so they wouldn't see any celebrity politicians. It was too much for the woman and her family. She cornered Ballard and gave him a mouthful. Some years later Ballard was in a mobile police patrol when rioters torched much of downtown Washington. Suddenly Ballard burst out laughing. "I don't see much funny about this," said his buddy. Ballard explained: "I'm thinking about a woman in Illinois who is sitting in front of her television set applauding as she watches this town burn down!"

Years after Jimmy Carter's presidency Capitol Hill veterans were still recalling the unprecedented steps he took, as president-elect, to curry favor with them. He met with the prestigious Senate Foreign Relations Committee soon after his election and astounded members by giving them his private telephone number in Plains, Ga. Then he handed out his private post box number where they could reach him without having the mail opened by the Secret Service. Before Inauguration Day, Carter met with the committee for a full day's discussion of world affairs. They were mightily impressed. In their collective memory, no one could recall another president-elect showing such consideration for senators and their staffs.

---

*Senate Foreign Relations Committee chairman Arthur Vandenberg warmed to his task so much that he told his wife she could have only two nights a week out. The rest had to be set aside for his Senate homework. His preparedness and easy-going manner won him the respect and affection of his staff through 22 years until he retired in 1950. Every morning the Michigan Republican used to walk over to the committee offices, put his feet up on a desk and exchange views in a relaxed style with the staff. Vandenberg's wife was just as popular. Though suffering from terminal cancer she insisted on going ahead with a staff Christmas party, telling her husband, "Arthur, I'm going to have that party if it's the last thing I ever do." She lived to take part in the festivities but died shortly afterwards.*

# PERILS & PITFALLS

———□———

*I have seen a presiding officer of the United States Senate amusing himself, while a senator was speaking, catching flies on the Vice President's desk.*

*-- Isaac Bassett, 19th century Senate assistant doorkeeper*

A drunk lawyer's conduct at a Prohibition rally in Texas led to a gunfight and the shooting deaths of four people, including Rep. John Pinckney (D-Tex.). Tension had been building for several years before the 1905 shootout in Waller County between those in favor of and against the sale of liquor. The slain congressman was a fervent Prohibition advocate. Matters came to a head when Capt. H. M. Brown, a prominent lawyer and one of the anti-Prohibition leaders, turned up at the rally tipsy and spoiling for a fight. When the smoke cleared Brown lay dead with a bullet through his heart. Pinckney, a county judge before his election to Congress, was felled by four bullets as was his brother, Thomas, with two rounds in his back. The fourth victim was a bystander.

———□———

House Speaker Joe Byrns (D-Tenn.) learned first hand how dangerous fishing could be in Mississippi. Invited down to open a new federal building in Hattiesburg, he later went fishing on an island where the water was quite rough. As the Speaker hooked a fish the boat listed. Byrns crashed against a hatch and fractured a rib.

Lamb's Biographical Dictionary of the U.S.

*Newton Curtis*

One of the tallest men ever elected to Congress lost an eye in the Civil War because he stood head and shoulders above every other soldier. Newton Curtis (R-N.Y.) won the Congressional Medal of Honor for bravery at Fort Fisher, N.C., where he was the first Union soldier through the stockade and led assaults even though wounded three times. When a Confederate general gave the order to fire a volley over the heads of the attackers to frighten them off, the bullets zinged above the enemy, with the exception of Curtis, who was almost 7 ft. tall. This fourth wound struck his eye.

*Elected as a Unionist to the 37th Congress in 1861, George Washington Bridges was on his way up from Tennessee to the nation's capital to be sworn in when he was waylaid and taken captive by Confederate troops. More than a year passed before he escaped. He arrived in Washington a week before the life of that Congress expired. Fortunately for Bridges, a former attorney-general of Tennessee, members voted to let him be sworn in.*

The letter from home was troubling for Rep. Cornelius Hamilton (R-Ohio.). His wife asked him to return from Washington quickly because she was uneasy over the strange behavior of their eldest son, Thomas. With only a few days to go before the Christmas recess of 1867, the congressman packed his bags. Back in the village of Marysville, where he had been a farmer, newspaper proprietor and lawyer, Hamilton took steps to have his son, 18, sent to an asylum for the insane. But while the papers were being processed Thomas came up behind his father in their barn, smashed his head with a heavy board and covered the body with corn fodder. He wounded his brother with an ax and chased his mother and others before being subdued. The murdered congressman had served a mere nine months in Washington.

A copy of the *Congressional Globe* folded in the coat pocket of Rep. Charles Van Wyck saved his life when a street thug stabbed him with a bowie knife. The blade slashed through Van Wyck's winter overcoat and jacket before being blunted by the triple folds of the *Congressional Globe*. The attempted assassination took place on Capitol Hill close to midnight in 1861 when the New York Republican was walking home from a friend's house. The congressman, 36, punched his assailant to the ground, then floored a second attacker who tried to knife him. As Van Wyck fired his pistol, wounding the first thug, a third member of the gang knocked the congressman unconscious before the three fled. Van Wyck lived 34 more years, serving as a senator from Nebraska after his move to that state.

The luck of the Irish saved freshman congressman Tip O'Neill from certain death when Puerto Rican nationalists opened fire in the House of Representatives in 1954. Moments after he left his seat on the floor of the House to meet with a reporter, the terrorists stood up in a spectators' gallery and sprayed bullets on unsuspecting congressmen. Amid screams and the moans of wounded representatives, one bullet slammed into the seat where the burly O'Neill had sat moments before. Though some of the injuries were serious, none of those felled in the bloody rampage died. The would-be assassins were captured and imprisoned. O'Neill went on to serve in Congress for another 32 years - ten of them as Speaker.

---

Time was when the President of the United States could walk alone through the snow-covered streets of Washington, D.C. and knock on the door of a home to surprise his friends inside. It happened when the 14th president, Franklin Pierce, called uninvited on Sen. Clement Clay, Jr. (D-Ala.) and his wife, Virginia. After taking off his hat, coat and scarf which shielded his identity from pedestrians, he gave Mrs. Clay a gift of a framed photograph of himself. Then the president, a former congressman at ease with himself, sat down before the fireplace and took an egg-nog. "Ah, my dear friends," he sighed. "I am so tired of the shackles of presidential life that I can scarcely endure it! I long for quiet, for this! Oh for relaxation and privacy once more, and a chance for home!"

W hen New Jersey Democrat Frank Thompson Jr. pulled up at a traffic light on his way to the Capitol a man leaned out of a truck and squirted sulphuric acid at him. It burned a hole in his shirt, slightly singed his arm, and left a scar on his auto. Thompson speculated the men in the truck may have been angered when he innocently cut across their path in the traffic. His wife, however, thought he had been deliberately targeted for supporting the labor reform bill of 1959. Before the vote he had received more than half a dozen phone calls threatening bodily harm.

Three Republicans reacted courageously as congressmen scattered for cover when an armed man stood up in the House gallery demanding 20 minutes speaking time. Diminutive Rep. Fiorello LaGuardia (R-N.Y.) dashed to the gallery to try and overpower the terrorist. Rep. Edith Rogers (R-Mass.), a 51-year-old former Red Cross worker, tried calming her panicky colleagues, telling them, "he won't hurt anyone." A former Marine officer, Rep. Melvin Maas (R-Minn.) rushed to a spot below the armed man, looked up and and roared, "You can't speak here with a gun in your hand. Drop it down here!" The young man complied and Maas, 34, caught the loaded and cocked pistol at the same time that LaGuardia and others in the gallery seized the would-be assailant. The 25-year-old department store clerk, who carried a list of grievances about conditions in the country, was led off by police. Maas later received the Carnegie Silver Medal for disarming the intruder.

# ISAAC BASSETT

———— ▯ ————

*What have I not seen in this, the most dignified body in the world.*

*-- Isaac Bassett, Senate page and assistant doorkeeper, 1831-1895*

No one in the 19th century knew the secrets of the Senate better than Isaac Bassett, who worked there for 64 years. The son of a Senate doorkeeper, Bassett was born in Washington, D.C. in 1819 and was only 12 when Sen. Daniel Webster appointed him a Senate page. Later he became a messenger and by the Civil War was promoted to assistant doorkeeper, a post he held until his death in 1895. Though unschooled and able to write only with a heavy reliance on the phonetic sound of words, Bassett began to record his unique observations during the 1880s. The following is a typical example of his writings:

*"Ex Senator Davis of Messissippe was a veary abl Senator. When he addressed the Senate he always was listend to with grate atention. Stued hie in the esteame of all of the Senators he was quite eleguen and spoke with grate force - and was veary kiend and shochebeal wile all of the officers and employe of the Senate often coueld me up to his seat and conversed - and generali wanted me to wate on him - I became veary mutch atactah to him and he to me. Sune after I was elected to the offic that I now howld I was acuised of saying that I liked Jefferson Davis a good President - this was during the rebelien in 1862 - two Senators - wone of them maed the remark that if he thought that I haid saed so he would cut my head right off (hole and laive).*

For 64 years Bassett observed then chronicled the drinking habits of 19th century senators. An edited sampling shows his keen eye untainted by any sense of righteous judgment:

*Silas Wright of New York .... would call me up to his seat just before he commenced to speak .... to go to the restaurant and get him a tumbler of gin and seat it on his desk. In those days it was thought nothing for senators to have a little stimulation when they spoke.*

*I have seen Sen. Phillips of Vermont so drunk that he could not walk. On several occasions he had to be taken out of the Senate chamber. But (he) never interfered with the deliberations of the Senate.*

*Sen. Linn was one of the most agreable senators. When sober (he was) liked by all of the senators. (He) would take his annual spree and had to be kept in his room at his boarding house (for) weeks at a time.*

*Sen. Rusk of Texas would go on a spree for weeks. (He) was very boisterous. Had to be led out of the Senate chamber by his friends. At times he was very vicious. Have known him to burst open doors of committee rooms and defy anyone to prevent him. When sober (he) was one of the kindest senators that I ever knew.*

*Sen. McDougal of California would get on sprees and stay away from the Senate for weeks. Sometimes (he) would come into the senate dressed in his riding suit, with whip in hand and large spurs on his feet. (He) was considered a very able man, frequently seen on the streets riding a white horse, (and) so drunk that he could not keep on his horse.*

*Sen. Saulsbury was very fond of going on sprees. I have great reason to remember him. He is the senator who drew a pistol on me while the Senate was in session.*

*Sen. Pierce of New Hampshire was always very pleasant when he was under the influence of liquor. He would come into the Senate chamber with a smile on his face and was very jolly to us boys, telling us stories.*

*Isaac Bassett*

*The Senate chamber was packed to capacity during one of the debates featuring Daniel Webster in the days when Isaac Bassett was still a page. By special permission of the lawmakers, female spectators had been admitted onto the Senate floor. Bassett accidentally trod on the foot of one of the ladies and she howled above the din, "You have killed me!" Bassett knew she must be exaggerating because pages, forbidden to enter the chamber wearing heavy shoes, instead wore pumps. Bassett turned to the stricken female and said, "I could not have hurt you very much." To his great embarrassment, the lady shrieked even louder, "But you have trod on my corn!"*

**S**en. David Davis of Illinois weighed almost 400 lbs. and loved to eat. When he was president pro tempore of the Senate he made it a habit at about 5 p.m. to call on a senator to move for adjournment on the grounds that dinner time had arrived. According to the ever-observant Bassett, "the Nays would have it but Sen. Davis always declared that the Ayes had it." The instant he announced the fraudulent outcome, Davis would leave his chair and lumber off in search of food.

When Sen. Leland Stanford (R-Calif.) gave each of the 14 Senate pages a Christmas gift of $5 each in 1888, Isaac Bassett was quick to take note because no other lawmaker had ever been as generous. The holiday spirit did not desert Stanford, a former president of the Central Pacific Railroad. On every succeeding Christmas he continued to flourish $5 bills for each of the  pages.

Isaac Bassett's cool composure saved his life when a tipsy Delaware senator drew a pistol on him at point blank range and threatened to shoot. It happened during the Civil War when Sen. Willard Saulsbury Sr. made derogatory remarks about President Lincoln and noted abolitionist Sen. Charles Sumner of Massachusetts. Saulsbury refused to take his seat when ordered to do so by the vice president. The presiding officer then ordered the sergeant-at-arms to take custody of Saulsbury for disorderly conduct but as he was absent it fell to Bassett to carry out the order. Saulsbury, a Democrat, drew his pistol and stuck it in Bassett's chest. Bassett saw it was not cocked and told Saulsbury he was only acting on orders and urged the senator to accompany him out so they could have a drink together. Saulsbury consented, grumbling, "Bassett, damn you. If you had put your hands on me I would have killed you." The senator pocketed the pistol but as they got to the door he pulled it out again and refused to leave. "You promised me you would

**Saulsbury, a Democrat, drew his pistol and stuck it in Bassett's chest.**

go out," Bassett coaxed. Unknown to both men, one of Bassett's sons was watching the drama from a spectators' gallery and was on the verge of jumping down to tackle his father's would-be assailant. However, Saulsbury relented, exclaiming, "I will go into my committee room and take a drink with you. But Bassett, I would have killed you. Damn you." Once in the committee room Bassett left the senator in the custody of the Capitol police and returned to the Senate chamber. Immediately Sen. Powell (D-Ky.) congratulated him. "Bassett, you managed that so damn well. If you and Saulsbury had got into a fight we intended, on this side of the chamber, to join in and break up this Senate - but you were too smart for us." The following morning Saulsbury asked Bassett if he had indeed drawn a pistol on him. When told that he had he said he had no recollection of the incident. A resolution to expel Saulsbury for his conduct was dropped after he apologized and said Bassett would be the last person in the world he would want to injure.

When Sen. Francis Blair (D-Mo.) summoned five pages to his desk and gave them separate messages Isaac Bassett. asked what he was up to. Blair said it was his way of finding out which of the five was the smartest. In spite of the senator's unorthodox ways, Bassett said "the little fellows" liked him.

*Isaac Bassett*

*Isaac Bassett's respectful subservience to senators cost him hard-earned money. One day a senator brought a broken suitcase into the chamber and asked Bassett to arrange to have the locks fixed. The assistant doorkeeper gave it to a page to take to a trunk-maker, who fixed it up for $1.50. Bassett carried the suitcase over to the senator's desk and told how much the repairs cost. The senator reached in his pocket, said he didn't have any change, and promised to pay him back the following morning. The next day the senator and Bassett saw each other but the legislator didn't mention anything about money. Bassett never recovered the debt because, as he wrote, "I was too modest to ask a senator of the United States for money."*

*Lobbying*

No category of people ranked lower in Isaac Bassett's estimation than lobbyists who frequently called upon senators in the Capitol. "Most of them are blackmailers," wrote the assistant doorkeeper. "They are so crafty and treacherous that public men, men of reputation or means, are always on the alert against them." Bassett noted that Sen. Chase of Ohio would never go out to meet either a male or female lobbyist without a witness being present. So many lobbyists were in the habit of crowding the halls and lobbies outside the Senate chamber and sending their business cards in to the lawmakers that several senators ordered Bassett not to let the pages transmit the cards.

Though remarkably perceptive and impressionable, Isaac Bassett was always aware of his educational shortcomings, reflected daily in his phonetic spelling and lapses in correct spoken English. As a young page he was once tutored by Sen. Thomas Hart Benton (D-Mo.) upon using ungrammatical speech. Benton had asked young Bassett to locate someone in the Senate chamber. After he found the person, Bassett pointed him out saying,"There he is, setting on a sofa." Benton got up, put his hand on Bassett's head, and gently corrected, "My boy, don't say that again. Hens set."

———— ▯ ————

**"In 1883 a senator sent me a letter by one of the pages with a $50 bill in it with the statement that I had been very kind to him in giving him one of the best seats in the Senate. He wanted me to receive it as a Christmas present. I returned it to him with the statement that I was an officer of the Senate and tried to treat all senators alike. As he was the one who spoke first for that seat, he was entitled to it. He was perfectly astonished and insisted on my taking it. I told him I could not .**

———— ▯ ————

*Two senators who whooped it up in an Indian war dance close to midnight moved Isaac Bassett to write: "What have I not seen in this, the most dignified body in the world." It was the last night of the session in 1862 and the sergeant-at-arms was out trying to round up absentee senators to make a quorum for consideration of an appropriation bill. Without warning Senators James Nesmith of Oregon and Henry Rice of Minnesota suddenly leaped from their seats and danced around the chamber half a dozen times, whooping and yelling while they stabbed at the floor with their canes. According to Bassett the performance, which amused other senators, was "well performed and showed that they understood what they were doing, both being senators from the far western states where they had witnessed many a similar dance performed by the Indians."*

*Though poorly educated, Isaac Bassett had a flair for crafting distinctive pen portraits. Witness a sampling of his compact descriptions:*

"Sen. Daniel Webster was a model of manly excellence. He looked every inch a gentleman. His body was strong and muscular, his chest full and broad, his head large and firmly set upon his shoulders. His manners were perfect. He never strode into the Senate but sauntered in as if personally unnoticed. He was so conscious of his power and had all of his mental resources so well in hand that he never was agitated or embarrassed. Before delivering a speech he often appeared absent-minded but on rising to his feet he seemed to recover perfect self-possession. This was aided by thrusting the right hand within the folds of his vest while the left hung gracefully by his side. His dark complexion grew warm with inward fire. His courteous and inward eyes would start from the cavernous depths and flash with inspiration, the huge brain in its mighty work forcing the perspiration in tiny rivulets down the palpitating temples. Yet in these tremendous demonstrations of intellect Mr. Webster was never dramatic in action. Even in the utterance of his most eloquent sentences his body was in comparative quietude. The magnificent eye alone burned. In all other respects repose seemed to be the normal condition of his magnificent frame."

"There was living in Washington in 1832 a singular woman - the widow of Captain Royall of the U.S. Army. She (Anne Royall) was homely in person, careless in dress, poor in purse and vulgar in manners. She had much shrewdness and respectable talents. She published books in which she praised extravagantly those who bought her book or gave her money and abused those who refused or had in any way incurred her displeasure. Some, through love of flattery and through fear of abuse, contributed to her support. She made senators and members of the House pay a dollar for a copy of her book but 'outsiders' as she called them, only 75c."

Sen. James Blaine is not stately and stylish but he can turn around quicker than any senator that I have ever seen. He is always ready with a robust wit that is effective though it lacks the special sting of sarcasm. He has a variety of attitudes and when he puts his hands in his pockets, for a brief moment he indicates the direction of his remark by emphatic (movements of his) nose and chin."

Sen. Henry Clay was tall and slender. His mouth was large, his forehead high. His style when speaking was peculiarly happy. His voice was deep and commanding. His action when speaking was graceful. I have never heard his equal as an orator."

Sen. William Rufus de Vane King of Alabama was a spare man. He was a bachelor. We all called him Miss Nancy. He was a courteous senator."

*A chaotic scene in the House of Representatives*

For the last 33 years of his life everyone who knew Isaac Bassett called him Captain even though he had never served in the military. The honorary title which stuck was conferred upon him during the Civil War when Senate employees banded together for the defense of the Capitol. Styling themselves The Hamlin Guards, they elected Bassett their captain. The organization's secretary and self-styled lieutenant was Arthur Gorman, a page who later served as a U.S. senator from Maryland.

———————🔲———————

**Isaac Bassett, writing in the 1880s: "In the days of Webster, Clay, Calhoun and Benton a man of wealth was thought no more of than a poor man. But now he is king- courted, followed, flattered and imitated. No man can be a cabinet officer and escape ridicule who does not entertain in a way that would exhaust his salary five times over."**

*The Senate barber was combing Isaac Bassett's hair when Sen.. Ingalls (R-Kan.) walked in and told the hairdresser, "See that you fix that hair alright. Do you know that Bassett is the handsomest man in the Senate." Though the assistant doorkeeper and the barber immediately took issue with him, the senator insisted, "that is the opinion of a good many expressed in my hearing."*

———————🔲———————

The press had a field day with Isaac Bassett when he reached 75 years old. By then he had served as a page and assistant doorkeeper in the Senate for 63 years. The silver-haired, erect and rosy-complexioned veteran of Capitol Hill brought smiles to many when he admitted to enjoying night sessions, "sitting up with the boys."

Was Andrew Johnson tipsy at his inauguration as Abraham Lincoln's vice president? Yes, say contemporary accounts, but only because Johnson was sick and had taken his doctor's advice to drink on the morning of the inauguration. Not so, according to Isaac Bassett, who personally handed Johnson the bottles of brandy and whiskey to relieve his fatigue and weakness from traveling all through the previous night. Bassett was with Johnson in the office of outgoing Vice President Hannibal Hamlin when Johnson said, "I will take a little whiskey." After drinking very little, Johnson left to be sworn into office in the Senate chamber. He then made such a long speech that senators began to tire. Bassett stepped up and whispered, "Mr. Johnson, it is time for the Senate to proceed to the portico to attend the inauguration of Mr. Lincoln." Johnson took a few more minutes to wind up then left in a procession with the senators, walking, according to eyewitness Bassett, "as straight as any of them." Bassett said Johnson did not drink in the Capitol again that day. When Bassett returned the bottles to their place of safekeeping he was struck by a remark of the man in charge: 'Why, he has not drunk any. The bottles are both full.' Bassett's conclusion: "Anything unusual in his appearance or manner was the result not of his drinking but of his exhausted physical condition from travel."

*Overheard by Isaac Bassett as Democratic Senators Eaton of Connecticut and Thomas McCreery of Kentucky sat down next to each other for the opening of the 1878 session:*

*"How many shirts have you?" asked McCreery.*

*"Two dozen."*

*"What! Two dozen," said McCreery. "I never had but three at a time and now I have but two and have lost one."*

*Bassett chronicled the remarks with characteristic detachment. "The above conversation," he scribbled, "created quite a laugh among the pages and your humble servant who heard it."*

U.S. Senate Collection

*Daniel Webster*

The kindly Sen. Daniel Webster used to seat the young Isaac Bassett on his knee and talk "in the most gracious manner" until the day it rained cats and dogs. Webster told the page to go out and summon a carriage but Bassett couldn't find one and made the mistake of returning with the bad news. "With a frown the severest and blackest I ever saw, and one which I will never forget," Bassett wrote decades later, "he put both his hands on my shoulders and pushed me from him. I thought I would sink through the floor. He then in the sternest tones ordered me to get him a carriage and not to return without one." That was the last time Webster ever lifted the page onto his knee. The next day Webster explained his fierce behavior to Bassett's father, saying he had done it for the boy's own good. For good measure, he charged the older Bassett with spoiling the boy. Bassett believed the frightful incident brought on his first gray hairs, which later turned snowy white.

$Q$uick intervention by Isaac Bassett prevented an angry page from thumping a senator. It happened in 1877 after Sen. James Blaine told the page to bring him his copy of the Manual of rules. When the boy brought back a copy of Thomas Jefferson's *Manual* the senator flew into a rage and began cussing. The page tried to explain that while there were two Manuals he had brought Jefferson's because it was the most frequently consulted. Indifferent to excuses, Blaine (R-Me.) swore even louder at the page. Bassett took one look at the quick-tempered, powerfully-built page and stepped in as he was about to punch the senator. Bassett pulled the boy away and out of the chamber, averting what would have been an unprecedented clash between a senator and a page.

*Sen. William Merrick of Maryland was probably the only man in Congress ever to ruffle Issac Bassett's feathers beyond endurance. Merrick occupied the desk closest to the Senate chamber's main door, where the right of entry was supervised by Bassett. Merrick could no longer stand the constant interruptions from members of the public gathering outside the main door and asking Bassett to summon the senator so they could speak with him. The Marylander remained seated but took to cussing Bassett for bothering him. The bearded Senate employee decided he, too, had had enough of Merrick's outbursts. One day they went through the familiar ritual with Bassett telling the senator he was wanted outside and Merrick giving him a mouthful. This time the stranger was deeply hurt when Bassett told him the senator would not come out. The next morning Bassett uncharacteristically told Merrick he would no longer take such verbal abuse. From that day on Merrick never swore again at the kindly Bassett.*

When young Isaac Bassett was still a page he was carrying a water pitcher to a senate committee room when he slipped and fell, cutting his hand on the broken glass. Hearing someone fall, Sen. Silas Wright of New York rushed out of the room, helped the boy to his feet, wrapped a towel around the wound then sent him home for the day. When the page told his mother what had happened, she exclaimed, "What a good man!" Bassett remembered the incident all his life because the cut left a permanent scar.

Senators looked to Issac Bassett for support in more ways than one. On one occasion, as Vice President Schuyler Colfax stepped down from the rostrum he was suddenly overcome by dizziness. Bassett was close by and rushed to catch the pale-faced presiding officer from slumping to the floor. The assistant doorkeeper assisted Colfax to the vice president's room where he rested for several days before returning to the Senate chamber.

# ELECTION GLIMPSES

———□———

*There's a terrible tendency here (in the Senate) to think that everything we do and say, or omit to do, is of world consequence. But you know full well that you can go across the street and the bus driver couldn't care less.*

*-- Sen. Philip Hart (D-Mich.)*

Even though House Speaker Nicholas Longworth was an Ohio Republican his closest congressional friend was Texas Democrat John "Cactus Jack" Nance Garner. The two inveterate poker players, who kept private barrels of whiskey in their Capitol hideaways, cemented their friendship even more when Garner became minority leader. Longworth picked him up daily in the Speaker's official limousine and together they drove to their offices on the Hill. Garner, sensing his party would shortly gain power and that he would be Speaker, used to jest that "our car will soon be all mine!" During the close elections of 1930, when it was uncertain which party would control the House, Longworth wired Garner, "Whose car is it?" Garner replied, "Think it mine. Will be pleasure to let you ride." The Republicans, however, held onto a razor-thin majority and Longworth kept his limousine. Just five months later, however, Longworth died of pneumonia. That same year special election victories returned the Democrats to power. They elevated Garner to the Speakership and "Cactus Jack" got the limousine all to himself.

The first Socialist elected to the House of Representatives was twice barred from taking the oath of office because congressmen said he had given aid and comfort to the enemy during World War 1. German-born Victor Berger, who edited a newspaper in Milwaukee, had stridently opposed U.S. entry into the war. A federal judge sentenced him to 20 years imprisonment for disloyalty but this was reversed by the Supreme Court in 1921. Having taken his seat in the House in 1911, Berger was barred by an almost unanimous vote of his colleagues in 1919, and again a month later after the electorate returned him with an increased majority. But he went to Washington for six trouble-free years after more victories at the polls.

———————————□———————————

Ephraim Blaine did not reach the exalted position of his son, James, who was Speaker of the House of Representatives, but he proved every bit as politically sharp in his own run for local judicial office in Pennsylvania. Though Ephraim Blaine was a Presbyterian, he had married a Catholic, which dimmed his chances of election. He did not object, however, when his wife's priest stepped into the fray with a saucy bit of humor. The priest's statement which tickled the fancy of the electorate and won their votes, read: "This is to certify that Ephraim Blaine is not now and never was a member of the Catholic Church; and furthermore, in my opinion, he is not fit to be a member of any church."

*The first woman elected to Congress also became the only legislator on Capitol Hill to vote against U.S. entry into both world wars. Soon after Jeannette Rankin, a suffragette and Republican, won election to the House of Representatives from Montana in 1916, she voted to stay out of World War 1. When the female pacifist won reelection in 1940, she again cast her vote against the declaration of war. After Rankin died in 1973, Montana honored her with a bronze statue in the U.S. Capitol's statuary hall, where each state is allowed to place only two statues of famous personages.*

*World War 11 veteran Laurie Battle returned home to Birmingham, Ala. to find his job in personnel management taken by someone else. Then he read about an upcoming congressional race and thought he'd rather be a congressman. He had written to his fiance from overseas asking if she would like to be a congressman's wife, half expecting her to reply, "which congressman?" The next step was finding out what qualifications were required of a congressional candidate. To his amusement, Battle discovered the biggest thing he needed to do was pay a $250 fee to the Democratic party. It was a sound investment. He won the election and three more after that.*

Rep. Charles Griffin (D-Miss.) was exhausted but it was an election year so he accepted the invitation to eat chitterlings at a school supper in Roxie before going on to speak in Meadville. He dropped a $20 bill in a plate and a girl loaded him up with chitterlings which he felt obliged to eat even though he disliked them. Griffin was so tired by the time he got to Meadville that he gave the worst speech of his life. Back in Washington he told of his misfortunes as he dined with fellow Southerners. "Well, Charlie," one of them jested, "did you like the chitterlings?" "You're damn right!" answered Griffin. "With 400 voters watching me eat them, I liked them!"

## UTAH

The Governor of Utah overturned George Cannon's landslide election to Congress after learning he was a polygamist with four wives who had borne him children. But Cannon, a Mormon, refused to go along when the governor gave the certificate of election to the defeated candidate, Allen Campbell. In 1882 the House of Representatives held an impassioned debate on Cannon's eligibility. "Polygamy is a disgrace to our civilization and offensive to the moral sense of mankind," thundered one member. Another demanded the exclusion of anyone from Utah "until it sends a representative for a law-maker who is not a notorious law-breaker." A forceful opponent damned polygamy as "odious" but cautioned his peers: "When you drag down polygamy take heed lest you involve the constitutional liberties of your country in ruin." By a vote of 123-79, the House decided not to seat Cannon. But it also disqualified the rival candidate, Campbell, and declared the seat vacant. Later that year John Caine won a new election and in 1883 was allowed to take his seat for the remaining two months of the 47th Congress.

*Congressman Harry Rusk told tall stories. In one of them he related how he cleaned up local politics in more than a figurative sense, while chairman of the Democratic committee in Baltimore, Md. There were apparently several slaughter houses close to polling stations towards the end of the 19th century. Sometimes, when the Democrats noticed a clutch of Republicans heading for the polling stations to vote, they would snatch an innocent bystander, rush him to the slaughter house, dip his head in the blood-filled vats and then chase him off in the direction of the polling station. Terrified by the gory spectacle, the Republicans would run off without voting. Rusk claimed he put an end to such scare tactics.*

The voters of Alabama liked John Sparkman so much they elected him to the House of Representatives and to the Senate on the same day in 1946. The feat has no equal in American history. Sparkman, a Democrat, had already served five terms in Congress and been nominated for another term when a vacancy arose in the Senate through the death of Alabama's Sen. John Bankhead, Jr. Sparkman opted for the Senate campaign but his name remained on both ballots. Victorious in the simultaneous elections, Sparkman promptly resigned his House seat to serve in the Senate.

In the musical chairs for a congressional seat from California, Medal of Honor winner Edouard Izac (D) beat Ed Fletcher (R) but six years later was trounced by Fletcher's son, Charles. There was an eerie parallel in the vote count. The first time around Izac got just over 69,000, the same amount young Charles polled when he won in 1946.

*Albert Gallatin*

One of America's most distinguished patriots, whose statue stands in front of the Treasury adjacent to the White House, was shoved out of the Senate when political foes discovered he had not filed his citizenship papers early enough. Swiss-born Albert Gallatin had served in the Revolutionary War, taught at Harvard and been elected to the Pennsylvania legislature before his election to the U.S. Senate. By that time he had lived in the new nation for 14 years. But Gallatin had not been a citizen for the minimum nine years to make him eligible to sit in the Senate. When he took his seat in December 1793 some politicians raised the legal technicality to oust him. Voting along partisan lines, his colleagues decided 14-12 to void his election. It was a minor set-back. Gallatin went on to be elected three times to the House of Representatives. He then served for 13 years as Secretary of the Treasury under Presidents Thomas Jefferson and James Madison. Gallatin rounded out his public service as American envoy to France and Great Britain.

——————————☐——————————

*Indiana Sen. Harry New was in the Capitol soon after losing a reelection primary when a visitor who had obviously lost her way asked him if he knew how to get out of the Senate. "Madam," said New bowing low, "I advise you to run in an Indiana primary."*

*Though almost a quarter of a million people voted in New Hampshire when Republican Louis Wyman and Democrat John Durkin faced off for a U.S. Senate seat in 1974, the result was so close that it took another election to produce a winner. At first it appeared Wyman, a five-term congressman, had won by a 355 votes. Subsequent recounts had Durkin ahead by 10 votes and then Wyman the victor by only two. The dispute spilled over into the Senate, where contested elections are decided. However, the lawmakers got bogged down over confusing ballot papers. Nine months after the election they threw up their arms and demanded a new, special election to decide the issue. The voters obliged, giving Durkin a convincing 27,781 edge over Wyman. "It was a long damn election night," said Durkin.*

Sen. Key Pittman (D-Nev.) was one of the most respected men in the land but when he died many Republicans cried foul. They thought he had passed away before reelection to a sixth term. It looked like a steal because he dropped out of sight four days before the Nov. 5, 1940 election. Actually, he was hospitalized with a weak heart but hung on with the aid of an oxygen tent. Pittman, who was president pro tem of the Senate and chairman of the Foreign Relations Committee, died five days after the election.

*Theodore Bilbo's death in 1947 spared senators the unsavory task of deciding whether he was fit to join them. Bilbo, a former Ku Klux Klan member and Democratic governor of Mississippi, had already been a senator for 12 years when his colleagues put a hold on his credentials. They refused to let him take his seat after reelection in 1946 until Senate committees investigated his dealings with war-time contractors and charges he had conducted a racist primary campaign. He was later censured for using his high office for personal gain but died before the other allegations were acted on.*

*James Shields*

*A*n Irish immigrant who survived a shipwreck on his way over to America, remains the only person to have been elected by three different states to the Senate. James Shields, a Democrat, won election from Illinois, Minnesota and Missouri. The former Illinois supreme court judge, who spoke Latin, French and Spanish, had also been governor of Oregon Territory and a hero in the war with Mexico before arriving in Washington, D.C. to take his Senate seat for the first time in March 1849.

To his consternation, the political opposition challenged his eligibility and sent him packing just nine days later. Though Shields had lived in the U.S. for more than two decades he had been naturalized only in October 1840, leaving him still 7 months short of having been a citizen for 9 years to make him eligible for the Senate. Shields won immediate reelection in Illinois and when October came around took his seat without objection. A decade later he was living in Minnesota when it was admitted to the Union and Shields won election to represent it in the Senate. After serving as a Brigadier General with Union forces in the Civil War, Shields moved first to California and then to Missouri, where in 1879 he triumphed again with election to the Senate. He is memorialized by all three states, with Illinois conferring the highest honor by placing his statue in the Capitol's exclusive Statuary Hall.

By the time Thomas Gerstle Abernethy got elected to the House of Representatives everyone called him Tom. It wasn't that way back in 1903 after his birth in Mississippi. For years everyone called him Gerstle. He found out why when his peers at school had a hard time pronouncing it and he asked his mother for an explanation. She told him his Daddy had worked as a salesman for the Gerstle Medicine Company in Chattanooga, named after a prominent local family. Old man Abernethy wanted to impress his boss by naming his son Gerstle. When Gerstle got into politics he spread the word that he wanted to be known as Tom. By that name he impressed the voters and won 15 terms to Congress.

Norman Dicks didn't think it was such a big deal winning election to the House of Representatives in 1977. He thought he had much more clout during eight years as a Capitol Hill aide to Sen. Warren Magnuson (D-Wash.). When people asked how he felt becoming a congressman, Dicks (D-Wash.) replied, "I never thought I'd give up that much power voluntarily."

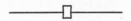

Rebecca Latimer Felton was a senator for a single day but she set three records which have stood since they were set in 1922. The 87-year-old Georgia Democrat, appointed before the winner of a special election was seated, became the oldest person and first woman to sit in the Senate. Her term was also the shortest ever served.

*T*hey hadn't seen each other in 20 years but still they recognized one another while taking oaths of office as new congressmen. Richard Bartholdt (R-Mo.) and Joseph Hendrix (D-N.Y.) had worked together as reporters on a Brooklyn newspaper in 1873 before Bartholdt moved out west to Hendrix's home state. But their careers continued on a striking parallel. Both were elected to school boards, and both became president, Bartholdt in St. Louis and Hendrix in Brooklyn. The two men did a double-take on meeting in the House chamber then celebrated with a drink for old time's sake.

Sen. Hiram Fong's wife gave him the silent treatment for three weeks solid when he did something she said would cost him the next election. The Hawaii Republican appointed his brother Herman to run the Honolulu office. Mrs. Fong said he was laying himself open to charges of nepotism. Not so, said the senator. Brother Herman was his alter ego. People would far rather talk their problems over with the brother of a senator than with a nondescript office assistant. Furthermore, Herman knew that everything he did would reflect on the senator. This would ensure he made correct decisions. Hiram Fong's obstinacy paid off. He won the next election.

———————□———————

A lot of congressmen had a good laugh over Vermont's duplicate returns from a 19th century presidential election. When the duplicates arrived in the nation's capital a joint meeting of the House and Senate refused to receive them. That's when they disappeared mysteriously. Suspicion centered on a Senate page, George McNair. Members of the House of Representatives confronted McNair but he refused to talk. The congressmen ordered him held in custody for several hours but then they decided it was not so important and let him go. According to the memoirs of McNair's superior, the page hung on to the returns even though he never opened them.

The 1876 presidential election was so close and hotly disputed that there was talk assassins might strike inside the U.S. Capitol. Samuel Tilden (D) polled more popular votes but Rutherford Hayes (R) won the presidency with an edge in electoral college votes. For the first time in congressional history, votes in from the states were carried from the Senate to the House under police guard and in strong wooden boxes instead of in the familiar packages tied with red tape. Shortly before senators and their staff walked over to the House chamber a friend of Senate assistant doorkeeper Isaac Bassett warned him of an assassination plot. The tipster said an unidentified gunman would assassinate Bassett as soon as he reached the Capitol rotunda. The gunman would then seize the wooden boxes and destroy the votes. "I told him I had no fears," Bassett wrote later. "I did not believe anything of the kind. The American people had more sense than to attempt anything of the kind. I was right. No attempt was made whatever."

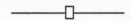

*Sen. Gordon Allott knew how to accept narrow electoral defeat because the former world champion athlete had once been pipped at the post in Olympic trials. "The only reason you should sit down afterwards and weep and wail is if you have not done your best," said the Colorado Republican. He lost his try for a fourth term in the Senate by a mere 9588 votes out of 905,502 cast. Allott compared the 1972 loss to his tryout for the U.S. Olympic team in 1928. Twice in one day he broke the world record for the 400 meter hurdles. But the next day Allott failed to make the team because all seven finalists shattered the world record. "You do what you can," he philosophized. "It is the same with the election. When it's over, it's over. You don't get a chance to run a race over."*

Rep. Wayne Aspinall (D-Colo.) was proud as punch after the Cherokee and Ute Indians made him an honorary member of their tribes. He knew it was a high honor and tribute to the great trust they placed in him during his many years as chairman of the House Interior and Insular Affairs Committee. Aspinall became close friends with Chief Jack House of the southern Ute tribe at Ignacio. They communicated through an interpreter though the chief always called Aspinall "Congress." Soon after Aspinall won the chief's precinct by 93 to 6 votes in the 1966 election, Chief Jack House called on Aspinall, as he always did just before the congressman's departure for Washington. The stoic-looking Jack House wore his familiar wide-brimmed black hat. His beaver-tipped braids hung down below his waist. Facetiously, Aspinall said he wanted to know the names of the six persons who voted against him so he could cultivate them and perhaps increase his majority. Chief Jack House listened carefully to the interpreter then stood expressionless for a long while. Finally he waved his hand and said, "Six?" He paused then announced who the mavericks were: "White men!"

The university reception for guest of honor Sen. William Borah (R-Idaho) was genteel and uneventful until two towering, unshaven lumberjacks burst in. One of them told the astonished guests, "We have come 100 miles to hear Bill Borah speak and a flat tire made us lose out. Now, by God, we are going to see him before he gets away." They cornered the five-term senator then running for his party's presidential nomination, and huddled with him for 15 minutes while amazed onlookers stood aside. Finally one of the lumberjacks, clutching a fistful of cocktail sandwiches, addressed the crowd. "Ladies and gentlemen, I hated to bust in on you. I like these sandwiches, even if they are a little skinny, but if you have any sense at all, you will vote for Bill Borah for president!" With that said the lumberjacks left. The boost for Borah failed to win him the nomination.

*Clyde Doyle couldn't decide whether to run for Congress. It was 1943 and many of his associates begged him to enter the race. The Californian sought his son's advice. He wrote a letter to Clyde, Jr., then a First Lieutenant in the Air Force on active service in the Aleutian Islands. The reply came back shortly. "Dad, you can't put on a uniform, but you can go to Congress and fight for a better world there by helping us make better laws so boys like me won't have to shed their blood again. It is up to the dedicated men of deep moral and spiritual convictions the world over, to bring about this longed-for peace and understanding on earth, men who will fight with all that is in them for the principles and ideals our country was founded on. So, go to it, Dad. I am with you all the way." The letter from his own flesh and blood was so encouraging that it tipped the scales. Doyle ran as a Democrat and won. Three weeks after he was sworn in he heard from the military. Clyde, Jr. had died in a plane crash.*

# TRADITIONS

———□———

*A simple, quiet courtesy is certainly the tone of manners in Congress.*

*-- James Fenimore Cooper*
*Author, Notions of the Americans*

The election of former Hollywood movie star George Murphy to the Senate in 1964 was good news for sweet-toothed legislators. The California Republican was never without a supply of candy in his desk on the Senate floor. He handed it out to anyone who wanted some, regardless of party affiliation. As word got around that Murphy stored sugared goodies, his back row mahogany desk came to be known as "the candy desk." When he left the Senate after a single term the tradition continued. To this day the senator who occupies that desk has a constant supply of candy inside for senators in need of a sweetener.

———□———

*Savory bean soup has appeared daily on the House restaurant menu ever since Speaker Joe Cannon's explosive decree in the summer of 1904. The granite-faced Speaker was so livid to find it missing from the menu that day, merely on account of the humid weather, that he ordered it restored and served up every single day. The soup, made up of white Michigan beans and smoked ham hock, remains the most popular course.*

*Throughout the 19th century senators sniffed snuff with an almost addictive frequency. The snuff box lay on the desk of the presiding officer and senators frequently walked up even in the middle of speeches to grab a pinch between their fingers. Millard Fillmore, presiding in 1852, got so irritated by these constant distractions next to his desk that he ordered snuff boxes attached to the walls, away from his rostrum. A tradition evolved through modern times of inviting freshmen senators at the beginning of every session to go through a light-hearted ceremony of taking a pinch of snuff. However, the number of sniffers dwindled and the custom disappeared into history books even though the snuff boxes are still kept filled.*

The coveted desk once occupied by Daniel Webster on the floor of the Senate is always reserved for the senior senator from New Hampshire. Though Webster had represented Massachusetts in the Senate, he was born and educated in New Hampshire. When Styles Bridges was New Hampshire's senior senator he discovered the desk in the Capitol basement. Carved on the bottom of a drawer were the distinctive initials, DW. Bridges occupied the desk until his death in 1961 when Sen. Norris Cotton claimed it. Shortly before retiring in 1974, Cotton got the Senate to agree to let all future senior senators from New Hampshire have the desk.

Nineteenth century senators cheated time by literally turning the clock back to finish their business. This way they didn't have to return to Washington for extra sessions. The unique tradition began in 1840 when an important appropriation bill scheduled for the Senate was delayed in the House on the last day of the session. The vice president, presiding over the Senate, ordered Isaac Bassett, then a messenger, to turn back the Senate clock twenty minutes. No one appeared to notice what Bassett had done as none of the senators queried his extraordinary activity. The bill arrived shortly afterwards, was acted on immediately, and beat the 12 noon deadline by two minutes.

In time, Bassett's ritual became the highlight of sessions about to wind up. All eyes were on him as he reached up with a broom handle to move back the brass minute hand of the giant clock. Once he moved it back too far and had to get up again to set it forward five minutes because the Senate was ready to adjourn. When challenged by one senator to explain where he received constitutional authority for his actions, Bassett said the vice president had sanctioned it and that was sufficient authority for him. Gradually public opinion questioned the unusual custom and even Bassett felt uncomfortable doing it. By the turn of the century the tradition had died out.

*Females lobbying senators in the U.S. Capitol*

*Two kinds of female lobbyists operated in the corridors of Congress in the view of a late 19th century chronicler of Capitol Hill. One was a "poorly-clad, nervous, wistful and frightened woman," horrified by her job. The other prowled the Capitol "bold and over-dressed and flashy." The shrinking violet was reported to find the personal audience with congressmen as disagreable as it was for legislators to receive her. Her only reason for pursuing her task was to further the interests of the cause at hand. But she "shrank at a rough word ..... and if she succeeds in getting anything it is because men take pity on her." By contrast, the brassy lobbyist was pictured as totally self-assured, with the implication that she would not withhold her favors if need be. "Maybe she influences some legislators," wrote the observer in* The Washington Star, *"but most of them being well-behaved married men are not subject to influences of this character."*

One hundred and sixty five years after John Adams gaveled the first U.S. Senate to order the little worn ivory gavel broke apart when Vice President Richard Nixon banged for decorum during a heated debate on atomic energy. The gavel, believed by some to be the original used by Adams, had seven years earlier been fitted with silver disks to each face to try and prevent it from splintering further. When the sergeant-at-arms could not find a new block of commercial ivory large enough to carve a replica of the shattered gavel, he turned to the Indian embassy. The Indians not only found the ivory, they fashioned the replica and that same year, 1954, presented it to the Senate. But senators were unwilling to part with a visible symbol of their link back to the first Senate session of 1789. The broken gavel therefore rests on the vice president's desk, next to the new gavel.

*Will Rogers, who brought chuckles to millions across the nation with his newspaper columns, once let on where he got so much to write about. "Congress," he said, "has been writing my material for years." Legislators loved the Oklahoman cowboy as much as anyone and proved it with a unique musical tribute after his death in a 1935 plane crash. When his statue was dedicated with traditional respect in the Capitol, the military band struck up the unexpected but familiar strains of* Home on the Range *and* The Last Roundup. *Rogers would have smiled wryly at the throng of congressmen honoring him. He had starred as one of them in a movie and quipped, "I have tried to live my life so that I would never become a congressman."*

When someone stole the holy Bible out of a drawer of the vice president's desk in the Senate chamber, assistant doorkeeper Isaac Bassett was beside himself. The musty Bible had been bought 53 years earlier by his father, who himself had been the Senate doorkeeper. Many senators sworn into office since 1829 had kissed the same Bible. According to Bassett the cover was marked "with the impress of their lips." The hue and cry, fanned by newspaper stories of the theft, failed to locate the treasured volume, whose cover bore the majestic gold stamp, U.S. Senate Chamber. Bassett missed the daily routine of unlocking the drawer at 9 a.m. to allow Senators to read the scriptures if they wished, and of relocking the same drawer at the end of the day. Three weeks after its disappearance, the Bible reappeared as mysteriously as it was taken. It was left on the desk of the secretary of the Senate without any covering note.

Carl Hayden was convinced that modern technology would help break Senate filibusters. The Arizona Democrat, who set a record 56 consecutive years in both houses of Congress, said more senators would be able to vote cloture because of improved communications and transportation. "When I first came to Washington," he told senators in 1949, "I traveled four nights on a sleeping car to get here. If I had been a senator at that time (1912) and had received telegraphic notice that a cloture petition had been filed, it would not have been possible for me to have reached here in time to vote. But today, because of the airplane, it is just an overnight journey from here to Phoenix. One can come from Paris, France, or Honolulu, in two days. So it is certain that from now on there will be a greater attendance of senators on such occasions."

**The rules were bent several times to accommodate old and ailing senators. A reporter who could not hear a speech made history in 1888 when he got permission to sit down at a senator's desk so he could be closer to soft-spoken Sen. William Evarts (R-N.Y.). That same year a sickly Sen. Joseph Brown (D-Ga.) was allowed to sit down while delivering his speech.**

*Vendor Clara Morris*

*T*he first souvenir and snack vendor inside the Capitol did so well that others attracted by the scent of her profits caused her fall from grace and eviction. Of French ancestry, Clara Morris arrived from New Orleans without fanfare or contacts during the Civil War. A combination of eccentricity and wiliness won her the first entrepreneurial foothold in the Capitol. She had attracted the attention of Vice President Hannibal Hamlin by unfurling the Stars and Stripes in the ladies gallery of the Senate chamber. Soon after, he befriended her. With his influence she won permission to open her business in a small recess of a corridor. The astute Clara then coaxed the Senate carpenter into making her first stall, entirely from his own spare pinewood. She did so well that she opened a larger business outlet in the space between the Rotunda and Statuary Hall. In time she owned several homes on Capitol Hill and property scattered elsewhere in Washington.

Others took note of her success and rival stalls sprang up like mushrooms. Gradually officials began to look askance at the unseemly mass of vendors. Protests reached newly-elected House Speaker Tom "Czar" Reed. Almost 30 years had elapsed since Clara had been allowed to sell her trinkets, guidebooks and souvenir pictures inside the domed building. This long tenure did not save her. Neither did her intimate ties to legislators and Capitol staffers, most of whom she knew by name and kissed on their hands. She was evicted together with all the other tradespeople. But the lure of the Capitol proved too much for old Clara. She regularly sat in the Senate galleries, explaining the history of the surroundings to attentive visitors.

# HATS OFF!

———◻———

*Blindness could not keep Sen. Thomas Schall, a former cowpuncher and bronco buster, off a horse. The Minnesota Republican didn't even balk at jumping 4 ft. high hurdles. He managed to judge objects and distances by having aides sound buzzers and bells at specific points. Blinded in both eyes by an exploding cigar lighter shortly after his marriage, Schall was the first sightless member of the House in 1915, before his election to the Senate. He had been plucky ever since his widowed mother gave him to a wealthy family. The boy ran off, joined a circus, then sold newspapers and shined shoes while sleeping on ironing boards in laundry rooms before working his way through college. Schall died in 1935 when hit by a car in the nation's capital.*

———◻———

Grover Ensley was astonished. As executive director of the Joint Congressional Economic Committee he had telephoned ahead for an appointment to see the cancer-stricken Sen. Robert Taft (R-Ohio). He needed the ailing senator's help on legislative work. Ensley knew from newspaper reports that Taft's days were numbered. Imagine his surprise when he walked in and saw the legendary "Mr Republican" next to an open Sears and Roebuck catalog, writing out an order for a new refrigerator for his home. Ensley was filled with admiration for Taft's spirit, though neither man knew just how close the end was. Taft died a few weeks later.

Three young war heroes with severe arm wounds became close friends during hospital convalescence and renewed contact when all later won election to the Senate. They were Philip Hart (D-Mich.), Daniel Inouye (D-Hawaii) and Bob Dole (R-Kan.) A mortar shell ripped off a large chunk of infantryman Hart's inner right arm when he landed on Utah Beach, France, on D-Day. Lt. Inouye's right arm was shattered, and later severed, by a German grenade in Italy during the closing weeks of the war. An exploding German shell, also in 1945 in Italy, cost Dole the use of his right arm. The highly decorated veterans met at Percy Jones Army Medical Center in Battle Creek, Michigan. Hart was the first to win election to the Senate, in 1958. Inouye followed four years later and Dole in 1968.

---

A measure of the widespread affection felt for Sen. Phillip Hart was gauged when an author sent his manuscript to Sen. Paul Douglas for review. The text described Hart as "a man widely regarded as the gentlest and kindest in the Senate." After reading the passage Douglas did something uncommon for a reviewer. He sent the galleys back with a note attached: "Don't say that Phil Hart is 'widely regarded' as the gentlest and kindest in the Senate. Just say he is."

*General Lafayette*

*W**hen Revolutionary War hero General Lafayette visited Washington, D.C. in 1824 an emotionally charged Congress voted him a gift of $200,000 and a township of 24,000 acres of land. It was not only appreciation for his military help half a century earlier but recompense for income lost and money spent during the war. In a formal letter to Lafayette, Congress said the gift was from "a people whose esteem for you can never cease until they have ceased to prize the liberty they enjoy." Replying, the French marquis described himself as "an old American soldier and adopted son of the United States - two titles dearer to my heart than all the treasures of the world."*

*The huge basket of fruit arrived unexpectedly from the presiding officer of the Senate, Vice President Richard Nixon. His gift was for the official reporters of debate. Nixon's accompanying card expressed appreciation for the hard work and long hours the Senate scribes had spent on the job. Veteran reporters could not remember any other vice president making such a thoughtful gesture.*

One of the very few women honored with a statue of herself in the Capitol walked at least six miles a day to save on street-car fares. It was one of the sacrifices educator Maria Sanford forced upon herself to repay debts from bad investments in real estate. A long-time professor of English at the University of Minnesota, she scrimped severely on food and transport to save money. Even though in her seventies, she walked three miles daily to grain cars at railroad yards where she collected floor sweepings to feed her chickens. Then she walked another three miles to teach at the university campus. The frugal lifestyle became habit. During World War 1 volunteer work around Minnesota, whenever the octogenerian traveled overnight by train she saved money for the war effort by paying for a seat instead of an expensive sleeper.

———————□———————

*O ne of the most courageous men ever to sit in Congress survived more than 200 operations for a crippling bone infection that left him confined to a wheelchair from the age of 15. David Hall's indomitable grit paid off when, at age 30, he became the first special student to graduate from the University of North Carolina Law School with an LL.B degree. A North Carolina attorney and cattle farmer, Hall, a Democrat, was elected to the House of Representatives in 1958 but died of cancer a year after taking his seat.*

*Thomas Jefferson*

Three weeks after British troops torched the Library of Congress in 1814, Thomas Jefferson offered his rare book collection as a replacement. Many of the elegantly bound volumes had been hand-picked by Jefferson while browsing through European bookstores when he was Minister to France. The range of titles reflected the retired president's wide interests. "There is, in fact, no subject to which a member of Congress may not have occasion to refer," he said in his offer. He guessed the collection would fill about 20 wagons and take two weeks to reach Washington, D.C. from his home at Monticello, Va. Congress liked the idea and paid him $23,950 for the 6,487 books.

*Revolutionary War hero Jesse Franklin cheated death when the hangman's noose broke and he galloped away to greater glory as president pro tem of the U.S. Senate. He had already won distinction on the battlefield when loyalists captured him. As they made a noose with his own bridle, Franklin warned, "If you hang me it will prove the dearest day's work you ever performed, for uncle Ben Cleveland will pursue you like a bloodhound, and he will never cease the chase while a solitary one of you survives." The loyalists went ahead with the hanging anyway. As if miraculously, the bridle broke and Franklin got away. Remarkably unpretentious as a senator and governor of North Carolina, Franklin cut the ruffles and frills off his shirts, claiming they did not suit the representative of plain people like his constituents.*

The man who roomed with President Kennedy during their undergraduate days at Harvard led a similarly spectacular life of achievement and glory before winning 11 successive elections to Congress. Boston-born Torbert "Torby" Macdonald roomed with JFK for four years, captained Harvard's football team, played professional baseball with a New York Yankees minor league team and then, in World War 11, won the Silver Star and Purple Heart as skipper of a PT boat that torpedoed five Japanese craft before being shelled itself off New Guinea. Macdonald first won election to Congress as a Massachusetts Democrat in 1954. He died in 1976 aged 58 after ordering life-support tubes removed during a serious illness.

The only U.S. naval officer captured by Germans in World War 1 was awarded the Congressional Medal of Honor and later served 10 years in the House of Representatives. Lt. Edouard Izac (D-Calif.) was taken prisoner aboard a German submarine which torpedoed his troop transport near France. On the voyage to a prisoner of war camp, Izac gathered vital information on the movement of enemy warships. Later, during an escape attempt, Izac, 26, jumped head first from a fast-moving train taking him from one POW camp to another. He was so severely beaten when recaptured that a German's rifle snapped in two as he smashed Izac unconscious on the back of the head. After more than four months of captivity, Izac escaped in a hail of bullets, clambered 120 miles by foot, then swam across the Rhine to safety in Switzerland. He sped to London and spilled the secrets of the German submarines to the commander of U.S. naval forces in Europe. But his courageous efforts came too late. The very next day German submarines began returning to their home ports flying white flags of surrender. The war was all but over. Izac was 100 years old when he died in 1990.

———————☐———————

*Rep. Charles Bennett ( D -Fla.) missed his first roll call in 20 years because he was home eating supper, thinking the House had adjourned for the day. He rushed back when he found out his mistake and heard members making speeches commiserating with him on the end of his record-breaking roll call presence. One congressman even asked the Speaker to have a rerun of the roll call so that Bennett's presence would be acknowledged. The Speaker politely turned this down saying "it would not be fair to the rules of the House." Bennett thanked his colleagues for their "very beautiful" concern, adding he was not dejected because luck had been with him all his life. Being absent for the first time in two decades was, he explained, "like a lot of things that come and go."*

Arizona's senior senator Henry Ashurst wrote one of the most eloquent tributes ever penned in memory of a colleague. When former cowboy and cattle king Sen. John Kendrick (D-Wyo.) died in 1933, Ashurst wrote a long letter of condolence to Wyoming's junior senator Joseph O'Mahoney, who had been a close friend of the deceased. "Amidst the din and sensation of politics in Washington, he longed for his shining Tetons and his gorgeous Yellowstone. His nostrils were always eager for the pungent odor of the wild sage, and his kindly eyes ever sought to descry the scarlet glory of the blossoming cactus..... The cowboy's work, like a particolored robe, is so woven about Senator Kendrick that a word describing the cowboy he so truly typified may not be out of place here. No belted knight in chivalry on heath or strand ever appealed with such allurement and glamour as did the American knights of the remuda.....The cowboy's life was one of severe isolation, but his work was not only made endurable but was even rendered pleasurable as well when he took refuge, as many, if not most of them, did, during their lonely rides, by entering into the realm of imagination, where ideal experiences are possible without objective restraint......and in this way a high percentage of the American cowboys became endowed with intellect and grace, fascination, and tremendous personal charm. Senator Kendrick symbolized the American cowboy - calm, steady, generous, fair, adaptable, industrious, and firmly devoted to the rugged old virtues which made our nation great and strong."

Sen. Hiram Fong's affection for Vice President Lyndon Johnson reached new highs when LBJ visited Hawaii to dedicate the East-West Center. Johnson invited Fong and his wife, Ellyn, to fly over in Air Force Two. The courtesy to Hawaii's Republican senator did not stop there. The luxuriously outfitted plane had a bunk-bed reserved for LBJ and another set aside for Lady Bird. Johnson offered the Fongs his own bunk, refusing to take no for an answer. But before moving off to sleep in the other bunk with his wife, Johnson even instructed them how to lie down together in the narrow bunk. "Why don't you put your head on this side and Ellyn put your head on the other side," said the solicitous Johnson.

———————□———————

*Though he served almost a quarter century in the senate, Missouri Democrat George Vest will always be remembered for his heartfelt tribute to man's best friend - the dog. When he was a young lawyer in the mid-19th century he represented a client suing another man who had killed his dog. Vest's speech was so poignant that for more than a century it has brought tears to the eyes of animal lovers. "A man's dog stands by him in prosperity and in poverty, in health and in sickness. He will sleep on the cold ground, where the wintry winds blow and the snow drives fiercely, if only he may be near his master's side. He will kiss the hand that has no food to offer ...... When all other friends desert, he remains ...... the faithful dog asks no higher privilege than that of accompanying him, to guard him against danger, to fight against his enemies. And when the last scene of all comes, and death takes his master in its embrace and his body is laid away in the cold ground, no matter if all other friends pursue their way, there by the graveside will the noble dog be found, his head between his paws, his eyes sad, but open in alert watchfulness, faithful and true even in death." Not surprisingly, Vest won his case.*

*Unknown to all but trusted insiders, longtime Speaker of the House Sam Rayburn could barely see his way around during his final years in office. Balding "Mr. Sam" was blind in one eye and saw only blurs through the other. He pulled off the remarkable feat of presiding over the House by leaning on others for help. Unable to see who rose to speak, Rayburn acted on whispered information from the parliamentarian. In the privacy of his office, the septuagenerian had staff narrate to him what he could no longer read. But even as his eyesight failed and cancer ravaged his body, the plucky Texan looked back on his life with deep satisfaction. "I am one man in public life who has achieved every ambition of his youth," he said. His boyhood dream, while attending a one-room school and working on his father's 40-acre cotton farm, had been to enter politics and become Speaker of the House of Representatives. When he died in office in 1961 he had amply fulfilled this early vision, serving for 17 years as Speaker.*

The woman defeated by Richard Nixon in a 1950 Senate race had many years earlier snubbed the Nazis by ripping up a contract to sing in European opera houses. Helen Gahagan Douglas, who also starred in Broadway plays, sacrificed top billing in Europe to protest the Nazis anti-Semitism. Douglas served six years in the House of Representatives before taking on Nixon for the vacant California Senate seat. A year before her death in 1980, Douglas, stricken with cancer, spoke by telephone hookup from her bedroom with a congressional hearing in Washington, D.C., and made a plea for cancer research funds.

When Ronald Reagan, 36, headed the Screen Actors Guild he came face to face with Richard Nixon, 34, then a member of the House committee on Un-American Activities investigating alleged communist infiltration of the motion picture industry. Reagan spoke harshly of the communists and their fifth column tactics but defended rights of free expression. "As a citizen I would hesitate, or not like, to see any political party outlawed on the basis of its political ideology. We have spent 170 years in this country on the basis that democracy is strong enough to stand up and fight against the inroads of any ideology." Asked if he had anything to say, Nixon replied curtly, "No questions."

George Bush started earnestly reading what were then called the women's pages of the Washington papers when he was a congressman and was so impressed that he got up in the House of Representatives to plug the recipe for a new cookie. It happened in 1969 when the future president read about the unlikely cookie made with a fish protein concentrate. General Foods heiress, Marjorie Post, had heard about the fish protein concentrate being touted by the Agency for International Development in its worldwide war on hunger. When AID officials sent the multimillionairess a cupfull by special taxi she promptly included it in a recipe for cookies, ate them for two days, then pronounced them "perfectly delicious." Bush, (R-Tex.), then chairman of the Republican task force on earth resources and population, instantly took her recipe to Congress. "I have been concerned about various methods of feeding the growing number of hungry throughout the world," he said. "Fish protein concentrate is one of those promising possibilities."

# PERMISSIONS AND CREDITS

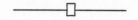

Grateful acknowledgment is made to the following for permission to reprint from previously published material:

Sam J. Ervin, 111, copyright holder and co-executor, Estate late Sam J. Ervin, Jr.: Rewritten excerpt from page 68 of *Preserving the Constitution*, The Autobiography of Senator Sam J. Ervin, Jr. Published by The Michie Company, Charlottesville, VA., 1984.

Harper & Row, Publishers, Inc.: Rewritten excerpts from pages 60 and 91 of *Tales Out Of Congress* by Senator Stephen M. Young. Copyright © 1964 by Stephen M. Young. Reprinted by permission of Harper & Row, Publishers, Inc.

Grateful acknowlegment is made to the following for permission to quote from unpublished material:

Office of the U.S. Senate Curator: the papers of Isaac Bassett and Donald Detwiler in the U.S. Senate Collection.

U.S. Association of Former Members of Congress; Mississippi Oral History Program, University of Southern Mississippi; Manuscript Section, Indiana Division, Indiana State Library: oral histories enumerated in Bibliography on pages 198-199.

Photographs, line drawings and silhouttes reproduced on the cover and in the inside pages were obtained from the following sources:

*Lamb's Biographical Dictionary of the United States.* Edited by John Howard Brown. James H. Lamb Company, Boston, Mass., 1900-1903. Vols. 1-7: pages 19, 26, 31, 32, 44, 67, 81 94, 103, 117, 132, 139, 163, 165, 181, 183.

*Library of Congress:* Cover and pages 24, 59, 66, 70, 71, 72, 73, 74, 77, 87, 128, 141, 175.

*New York Public Library:* Prints Division, Astor, Lenox and Tilden Foundations Page 68.

*U.S. Senate Collection:* Cover and pages 47, 54, 61, 65, 69, 80, 106, 116, 124, 126, 131, 146, 148, 149, 152, 155, 173, 174, 178.

# BIBLIOGRAPHY

———⟦⟧———

**Books:**

*Annals of The Congress of the United States: debates and proceedings of the Congress of the United States 1789-1824.* Gales & Seaton, Washington, D.C. 1834-1856. Multiple volumes.

Anonymous author. *The Mirrors of Washington.* G.P. Putnam's Sons, N.Y. 1921.

Bailey, Thomas A. *A Diplomatic History of the American People.* Prentice-Hall, Inc. Englewood Cliffs, N.J. 1970.

Baker, Richard Allan. *The Senate of the United States.* Robert E. Krieger Publishing Company, Malabar, Fla., 1988.

Bartholdt, Richard. *From Steerage to Congress.* Dorrance & Company, Philadephia, Pa., 1930.

Bemis, Samuel Flagg. *John Quincy Adams and the Union.* Alfred A. Knopf, N.Y. 1956.

*Biographical Directory of the United States Congress 1774-1989*, Bicentennial Edition. U.S. Government Printing Office, Washington, D.C. 1989.

*Biographical History of North Carolina from Colonial Times to the Present.* Editor-in-Chief Samuel A. Ashe. Charles L. Van Noppen, Greensboro, N.C. 1906. Vol. 4.

Brough, James. *Princess Alice - A Biography of Alice Roosevelt Longworth.* Little, Brown & Co. Boston, Mass. 1975.

Bruce, William C. *John Randolph of Roanoke 1773-1833.* G.P. Putnam's Sons, N.Y. 1922.

Burton, Katherine. *Three Generations: Maria Boyle Ewing, Ellen Ewing Sherman, Minnie Sherman Fitch.* Longmans, Green and Co., N.Y. 1947.

Byrd, Robert C. *The Senate 1789-1989. Addresses on the History of the United States Senate.* U.S. Government Printing Office, Washington, D.C. 1988. Vol. 1 Bicentennial Edition.

Chamberlin, Hope. *A Minority of Members - Women in the U.S. Congress.* Praeger Publishers, N.Y. 1973.

Cheney, Richard & Lynne. *Kings of the Hill.* Continuum, N.Y. 1983.

Childs, Marquis. *I Write From Washington.* Harper & Brothers, N.Y. 1942.

Christopher, Maurine. *America's Black Congressmen.* Thomas Y. Crowell Company, N.Y. 1971.

*Circular Letters of Congressmen to their Constituents 1789-1829.* Edited by Noble E. Cunningham, Jr. The University of North Carolina Press, Chapel Hill, N.C. 1978. Vol. 1.

Clay-Clopton, Virginia. *A Belle of the Fifties.* Doubleday, Page & Co., N.Y. 1904.

*Congressional Record: proceedings and debates of the Congress.* U.S. Government Printing Office, Washington, D.C. 1874 to present time. Multiple volumes.

*Congressional Quarterly's Guide to U.S. Elections.* Congressional Quarterly Inc., Washington, D.C., 1975.

Coolidge, Louis Arthur and Reynolds, James Burton. *The Show At Washington.* Washington Publishing Company, Washington, D.C. 1894.

Cooper, James Fenimore. *Notions of the Americans picked up by a travelling bachelor.* Carey, Lea & Carey, Philadelphia, Pa. 1828.

Cotton, Norris. *In The Senate: amidst the conflict and the turmoil.* Dodd, Mead & Company, N.Y. 1978.

Cullom, Shelby M. *Fifty Years of Public Service.* A.C. McClurg & Co., Chicago, Ill. 1911.

Currie, James T. *The United States House of Representatives.* Robert E. Krieger Publishing Company, Malabar, Fla., 1988.

Daniels, Jonathan. *The Randolphs of Virginia.* Doubleday, N.Y. 1972.

Davis, Burke. *Old Hickory - A Life of Andrew Jackson.* Dial Press, N.Y. 1977.

Dawes, Charles, G. *Notes as Vice President 1928-1929.* Little, Brown and Company, Boston, Mass. 1935.

Dawidoff, Robert. *The Education of John Randolph.* W.W. Norton & Company, N.Y. 1979.

Depew, Chauncey, M. *My Memories of Eighty Years.* Charles Scribner's Sons, N.Y. 1922.

*Dictionary of American Negro Biography.* Edited by Rayford W. Logan and Michael R. Winston. W.W. Norton & Company, N.Y. 1982.

*Drew Pearson Diaries 1949-1956,* edited by Tyler Abell. Holt, Rinehart and Winston, N.Y.

Dyer, Oliver. *Great Senators of the United States Forty Years Ago.* Robert Bonner's Sons, N.Y. 1889.

Eckloff, Christian. *Memoirs of a Senate Page 1855-1859.* Broadway Publishing Co. N.Y. 1909.

Flanders, Ralph E. *Senator from Vermont.* Little, Brown and Company. Boston, Mass. 1961.

Foraker, Joseph Benson. *Notes of a Busy Life.* Stewart & Kidd Company, Cincinnati, Ohio, 1916. Vol. 2.

Foraker, Julia. *I Would Live It Again.* Harper & Bros, N.Y. 1932.

Galloway, George B. *History of the House of Representatives.* Thomas Crowell Co., N.Y. 1976.

Goode, James M. *Best Addresses, A Century of Washington's Distinguished Apartment Houses.* Smithsonian Institution Press, Washington, D.C. 1988.

Gouverneur, Marian. *As I Remember.* D. Appleton & Co., N.Y. 1911.

Grund, Francis J. *Aristocracy in America.* Richard Bentley, London. 1839.

Haynes, George H. *The Senate of the United States.* Russell & Russell, N.Y. 1960.

Hinds, Asher C. *Hinds Precedents of the House of Representatives.* U.S. Government Printing Office, Washington, D.C. 1907. Vols. 1 & 2.

*History In The House* (Newsletter). Office for the Bicentennial, U.S. House of
　　　Representatives, Washington, D.C. Multiple issues.

Isaacs (Izac), Edouard. *Prisoner Of The U-90.* Houghton, Mifflin, Boston, Mass. 1919.

James, Marquis. *Mr. Garner of Texas.* The Bobbs-Merrill Company, Indianapolis &
　　　N.Y. 1939.

Jones, Rochelle & Woll, Peter. *The Private World of Congress.* The Free Press,
　　　N.Y. 1979.

*Lamb's Biographical Dictionary of the United States.* James H. Lamb Co., Boston, Mass.
　　　1900. Multiple volumes.

Langley, John W. *They Tried To Crucify Me or The Smoke-Screen of the Cumberlands.*
　　　John W. Langley, Pikeville, Ky. 1929.

*Medal of Honor Recipients 1863-1978.* Prepared by the Committee on Veterans'
　　　Affairs, U.S. Senate. U.S. Government Printing Office, Washington, D.C.
　　　1979.

Mesta, Perle. *Perle - My Story.* McGraw-Hill, N.Y. 1960.

Morgan, Anne Hodges. *Robert S. Kerr: The Senate Years.* University of Oklahoma
　　　Press, 1977.

Murdock, Myrtle Cheney. *Constantino Brumidi: Michelangelo of the United States
　　　Capitol.* Monumental Press, Washington, D.C. 1950.
Pilat, Oliver. *Drew Pearson - An Unauthorized Biography.* Harper's Magazine
　　　Press, N.Y. 1973.

Poore, Benjamin Perley. *Perley's Reminiscences of Sixty Years in the National Metropolis.*
　　　Hubbard Bros., Philadelphia, Pa. 1886, Vols. 1 & 2.

Porter, Sarah Harvey. *The Life & Times of Anne Royall.* The Torch Press book shop,
　　　Cedar Rapids, Iowa. 1909.

Prentice, George, D. *Biography of Henry Clay.* John Jay Phelps, N.Y. 1831.
　　　Second Edition, Revised.

*Preserving the Constitution: The Autobiography of Senator Sam J. Ervin, Jr.*
The Michie Company, Charlottesville, Va. 1984.

*Register of Debates in Congress: comprising the leading debates and incidents of the Congress, 1824-37.* Gales & Seaton, Washington, D.C. Multiple volumes.

Riedel, Richard Langham. *Halls of the Mighty: my 47 years at the Senate.*
Robert B. Luce, Washington, D.C. 1969.

Robertson, Ignatius Loyola. *Sketches of Public Characters.* E. Bliss, N.Y. 1830.

Rogers, Lindsay. *The American Senate.* Alfred A. Knopf, N.Y. 1926.

Roper, Daniel C. with Lovette, Frank H. *Fifty Years of Public Life.* Duke University Press, Durham, N.C. 1941.

Royall, Anne. *Sketches of History, Life, And Manners in the United States.*
Johnson Reprint Corporation, N.Y. 1826.

Saund, Dalip Singh. *Congressman from India.* E.P. Dutton and Company, Inc.
N.Y. 1960.

*Senate History* (Newsletter). U.S. Senate Historical Office, Washington, D.C.
Multiple issues.

Sherman, Thomas. *Twenty Years With James G. Blaine - Reminiscences by his Private Secretary.* The Grafton Press, N.Y. 1928.

Snyder, Charles McCool. *Dr. Mary Walker: The Little Lady in Pants.* Arno Press, N.Y.
1974.

Stealey, O.O. *Twenty Years In The Press Gallery.* Publishers Printing Company, N.Y.
1906.

Stephen M. Young. *Tales Out Of Congress.* Harper & Row, N.Y. 1964.

Swanberg, W.A. *Sickles the Incredible.* Charles Scribner's Sons, N.Y. 1956.

Swanstrom, Roy. *The United States Senate 1787-1801: a dissertation on the first fourteen years of the upper legislative body.* U.S. Government Printing Office, Washington, D.C. 1985.

*The Congressional Cook Book.* The Congressional Club, Washington, D.C. 1965.

*The Congressional Globe: containing debates and proceedings of the Congress 1833-73.* Office of the Congressional Globe, Washington, D.C. 1836-73. Multiple volumes.

*The Congressional Term - When Does It Begin And End?* Compiled by Henry M. Rose. U.S. Government Printing Office, Washington, D.C. 1911.

*The Letters of John Fairfield.* Edited by Arthur G. Staples. Lewiston Journal Co., Lewiston, Me. 1922.

*The Smithsonian Institution: Documents Relative to its Origin and History 1835-1899.* Compiled and Edited by William Jones Rhees. Government Printing Office, Washington, D.C. 1901. Vol. 1.

Todd, Charles Burr. *The Story of Washington, the National Capital.* G.P. Putnam's Sons, N.Y. 1889.

Trollope, Frances. *Domestic Manners of the Americans.* Edited, with a History of Mrs. Trollope's Adventures in America, by Donald Smalley. Alfred A. Knopf, N.Y. 1949.

Van Deusen, Glyndon, G. *The Life of Henry Clay.* Greenwood Press, Westport, Conn. 1979.

Watson, James E. *As I Knew Them.* The Bobbs-Merrill Company, Indianapolis & N.Y. 1936.

Webb, Terrell D. *Washington Life - Journal of Ellen Maury Slayden 1897-1919.* Harper & Row, N.Y. 1962.

Wharton, Anne. *Social Life in the Early Republic.* Benjamin Blom, N.Y. 1902, 1969.

Williams, T. Harry. *Huey Long.* Alfred A. Knopf, N.Y. 1969.

Wilson, Rufus Rockwell. *Washington The Capital City.* J.B. Lippincott Company, 1902. Vol. 1.

**Papers:**

U.S. Senate Collection
  Isaac Bassett Papers.
  Donald Detwiler Papers.

**Oral Histories:**

U.S. Senate Historical Office

Attig, Francis J. Reporter of U.S. Senate debates.
Ballard, Leonard H. Inspector, U.S. Capitol Police
Detwiler, Donald J. U.S. Senate page.
Ensley, Grover W. Executive Director, Joint Economic Committee, U.S. Congress.
Holt, Pat M. Chief of Staff, U.S. Senate Foreign Relations Committee.
Little, Franklin, J. U.S. Senate page.
Marcy, Carl M. Chief of Staff, U.S. Senate Foreign Relations Committee.
McClure, Stewart E. Chief Clerk, U.S. Senate Committee on Labor & Public Welfare.
Reid, Warren Featherstone. Aide to U.S. Senate president *pro tem* Warren Magnuson.
Riddick, Floyd M. Parliamentarian, U.S. Senate.
Ridgely, William A. Chief Financial Clerk and Assistant Secretary, U.S. Senate.
St. Claire, Darrell. Chief Clerk and Assistant Secretary, U.S. Senate.
Watt, Ruth Young. Chief Clerk, U.S. Senate Permanent Subcommittee on Investigations.
Wilcox, Francis O. Chief of Staff, U.S. Senate Foreign Relations Committee.

**Oral Histories:**

U.S. Association of Former Members of Congress

Gordon Allott (R-Colo.); Leslie Arends (R-Ill.); Wayne Aspinall (D-Colo.); William Ayres (R-Ohio); Laurie Battle (D-Ala.); Frank Becker (R-N.Y.); Catherine May Bedell (R-Wash.); Wallace Bennett (R-Utah); Reva Bosone (D-Utah); John Bricker (R-Ohio); Emanuel Celler (D-N.Y.); Marguerite Church (R-Ill.); William Cole (R-N.Y.); William Colmer (D-Miss.); Robert Denney (R-Neb.); William Dorn (D-S.C.); Emily Douglas (D-Ill.); Charles Fletcher (R-Calif.); Hiram Fong (R-Hawaii); J. Allen Frear (D-Del.); Peter Frelinghuysen, Jr. (R-N.J.); Charles Goodell (R-N.Y.); Edith Green (D-Ore.); Martha Griffiths (D-Mich.); Charles Gubser (R-Calif.); Leonard Hall (R-N.Y.); Julia Hansen (D-Wash.); Porter Hardy, Jr. (D-Va.); Brooks Hays (D-Ark.); Patrick Hillines (R-Calif.); Walter Judd (R-Minn.); Hastings Keith (R-Mass.); Edna Kelly (D-N.Y.); Phillip Landrum (D-Ga.); Rodney Love (D-Ohio); Ray Madden (D-Ind.); William Mailliard (R-Calif.); Gale McGee (D-Wyo.); George Outland (D-Calif.); James Roosevelt (D-Calif.); Leverett Saltonstall (R-Mass.); Henry Schadeberg (R-Wis.); Katharine St. George (R-N.Y.); John Terry (R-N.Y.); Albert Vreeland (R-N.J.);

Stuyvesant Wainwright 11 (R-N.Y.); Otha Wearin (D-Iowa); William Widnall (R-N.J.); John Williams (R-Del.); Chase Going Woodhouse (D-Conn.).

**Oral Histories:**

Mississippi Oral History Program, University of Southern Mississippi
Thomas Gerstle Abernathy (D-Miss.); Charles Griffin (D-Miss.); John Bell Williams (D-Miss.).

**Oral Histories:**

Manuscript Section, Indiana Division, Indiana State Library
E. Ross Adair (R-Ind.).

**Congressional Hearings:**

Reagan, Ronald. *Communist Infiltration of the Motion Picture Industry.* Hearings before the Committee on Un-American Activities, House of Representatives, October, 23, 1947. U.S. Government Printing Office, Washington, D.C. 1947.

Walker, Dr. Mary E. *Woman Suffrage.* Hearings before the Committee of the Judiciary, House of Representatives, February 14, 1912. U.S. Government Printing Office, Washington, D.C. 1912.

**Magazines:**
Time
Newsweek

**Newspapers:**
Baltimore Sun
Capital News (Boise, Idaho)
Evening Star (Washington, D.C.)
Herald (Sylva, N.C.)
National Intelligencer
New York Daily Tribune
New York Times
Philadelphia Record
The Sun (Portland, Ore.)
The Week (New London, Conn.)
Wall Street Journal
Washington Post

# He may be a good kid with a bad case of Tourette Syndrome

Strange behavior may be a signal of a difficult-to-diagnose disorder called Tourette Syndrome.

Symptoms may include sudden body movements, tics, uncontrollable, repeated twitches and jerks, or shrill yelping noises.

Parents will share your concern. We can help.

For more information, contact:
The Tourette Syndrome Association
42-40A Bell Boulevard, Bayside, N.Y. 11361
Telephone: 718-224-2999

**Tourette Syndrome Association
Knowing what you have - is knowing what to do.**